In His Hands

In His Hands

Towards a Theology of Healing

DAVID DALE

Foreword by Tom Smail

daybreak
London

First published in 1989 by
Daybreak
Darton, Longman and Todd Ltd
89 Lillie Road, London SW6 1UD

British Library Cataloguing in Publication Data

Dale, David
  In his hands: towards a theology of healing.
  1. Christianity. Spiritual healing
  I. Title
  615.8'52

  ISBN 0–232–51851–3

Phototypeset by Input Typesetting Ltd,
London SW19 8DR
Printed and bound in Great Britain by
Courier International Ltd, Tiptree, Essex

To my grandchildren –
in faith, hope and love

Contents

Acknowledgement

Biblical references, except where otherwise stated, are to the Revised Standard Version of the Bible, copyrighted 1971 and 1952 by the Division of Christian Education of the National Council of the Churches of Christ in the USA.

Foreword

It takes many ingredients to produce a good book about the ministry of healing; in this book David Dale shows that he has an ample supply of most of them.

Like the charismatics he has a large and faithful expectation of what the living God can do in Christ for all who turn to him in their need, borne out by a long experience of what has actually happened to those with whom he has worked and prayed. Again and again the book comes alive with highly credible descriptions of the good things he has seen God do.

With the evangelicals he has a respect for the word of God in both Christian senses. The healing ministry in which he participates is in the name of Jesus, the Father's living Word, and he warns us against straying into the grey and dangerous areas where that name is not invoked or honoured. Throughout he seeks to base his conclusions on the written word of Scripture and there are some fresh insights into familiar passages, notably what he has to say about Paul's thorn in the flesh.

With the catholics David knows the value of the sacramental sign and he has some interesting things to say about both the laying on of hands and anointing.

David promises that the theology he offers will be practical rather than academic and so indeed it is. Nevertheless it is always clear that he has done a lot of reading and still more thinking about his subject, so that he knows what the real questions are and what answers to give to them. Sometimes indeed he speaks with the almost prophetic authority of a man who over many years has been far in the counsel of God.

He can distinguish what is primary from what is secondary and his wide sympathies enable him to look for and find the best in all the types of healing ministry that are being offered today. When he occasionally turns from affirmation to questioning, it is because his sharpened sensitivity has sensed dangers that enthusiastic riders of bandwagons easily miss: his warnings in my judgement deserve to be heeded, not least because they are so few.

The book shows a none too common blend of theory and practice, of enthusiasm and caution, of disciplined thought and mature experience. From start to finish David is concerned as a Christian minister to keep us mindful of the difference between being cured and being healed, and of how many have the one without the other. The writing has a pastoral gentleness and graciousness about it that are themselves calming and healing and are part of that *shalom* which is David's main theme and which he evidently knows from the inside. The result is that having read the book, you are left feeling that you know and can trust the man that wrote it.

Of course the book raises questions that it does not answer and just sometimes prods us into finding different answers of our own. But that is what a good book always does, especially a book by a man who knows that when we are talking about healing, we are talking about mystery, because we are talking about God.

TOM SMAIL

Preface

In one of her last reports as Religious Correspondent of the BBC, Miss Rosemary Harthill said that she felt that there was obvious need for the Church to pay more serious attention to its healing ministry. At the same time she expressed anxiety about forms of healing ministry which left people feeling confused and disappointed, and services for healing where expectations of healing were quickened but not fulfilled and people were left with an added burden of guilt.

Lord Coggan, former Archbishop of Canterbury, in his Henry Cooper Memorial Lecture, referred to a resolution of the Lambeth Conference of 1978 which affirmed that to neglect the healing ministry was 'to diminish our part in Christ's total redemptive activity'. He went on to call for greater teaching in this area; for 'to try to exercise a healing ministry where there has been no preparatory teaching is to act like a bull in a china-shop'.

But what is this teaching to be? With one or two significant exceptions, our systematic theologians remain silent on this theme. One can understand this, for it is not a subject that lends itself to neat formulations.

To speak of healing is, almost by definition, to speak of sickness and suffering and it is especially difficult to speak about such things with balance and with truth. For most of us have known difficult experiences in relation to sickness and suffering and in some ways bear the marks of that pain. There are those who feel that they must defend sickness as a kind of blessing. Others are inclined to question the faith of those who go unhealed, as though they felt it necessary to defend God's honour. There are many more who acknowledge that they are completely bewildered by the whole question.

We must acknowledge that sickness and suffering are a mystery, a part of the mystery of evil, and a mystery that has baffled the finest minds of Christendom in every age. Anything that offers a simple solution therefore is likely to be only partially true.

Much the same can be said about Christian healing. Some within the Church, frequently under the pressure of an anti-intellectual bias, preach a simple doctrine of universal healing on the promise of faith and do so with great power and effect, or so it seems. Others, within a more liberal and reflective tradition, speak about Christian healing, if at all, with great caution and little power. Surely, if these things are of God, then there must be a way of speaking of them which is courageous in faith but also in touch with reality and which has about it the ring of truth.

This book is intended for ministers and interested laypeople who may have theological and other problems about the Church's healing ministry. It attempts to examine some of the theological assumptions which underlie various aspects of the Christian healing movement in the Church today. I have deliberately chosen to paint on a broad canvas. I hope that the reader will accept the limitations in depth and detail that this strategy imposes. In writing I have become more and more aware of the inadequacies in my biblical and theological background. Having spent over thirty-five years as minister in a local church and twenty of those in large and demanding churches, my time for wide reading has been limited. I trust that the reader will pardon the resulting failures and omissions. At the same time, I would pay tribute to the many friends and colleagues who have influenced my thinking in these matters over the years and, in particular, the late Dr Robert Lambourne, who guided my thinking for a brief period until his all too untimely death in 1972. He brought to so many a prophetic gift and spirit which it is a delight to cherish but impossible to repay.

The continuing and caring (if not always uncritical) support of my wife and two sons is implied, if not described, in the dedication.

Healing Ministry in the Church Today

With the quickening of interest in the Church's healing ministry during the last few years, there is today some indication of a real desire to look more carefully at its theological roots. That is largely the reason for adding to the considerable amount of writing on this theme. As I am working on a broad canvas, it is possible to give only pointers rather than a comprehensive survey of this area of the Church's ministry.

My own interest in Christian healing was quickened by wartime experiences in India and the Middle East. There one learned that medicine as practised in the West did not have all the answers to the ills that trouble human beings; that a greater understanding of who and what we are, that prayer and a deeper reliance on the grace and goodness of God, might all contribute considerably to human health and happiness.

After the fall of France in 1940, I found it increasingly difficult to justify my reserved occupation as a theological student and left college to serve as a radio officer in the Merchant Navy. There I found that I was often expected to act as a kind of unofficial chaplain. One day at breakfast there was much discussion about an Indian greaser who was apparently quite ill but no one knew the exact nature of the illness. The chief engineer invited me to go with him to investigate. On the way to the sick man's quarters we met the headman and asked what was wrong. 'Oh, very sick, sahib, very sick, we think he die.'

When we reached the seaman's cabin, we found him looking desperately ill and surrounded by Indians who were chanting and throwing rice on his bunk, as if to prepare for his fairly immediate demise. Arrangements were quickly made to have the sick man taken from that atmosphere and given hospital accommodation away from the other Indians. Within forty-eight hours the seaman had recovered sufficiently to return to work again. On enquiring further, we discovered that he had fallen over a bucket in the engine-room and, as we would have said, sprained his ankle. But this man thought that someone had put an evil spirit on him and that he was about to die. If he had been left in that atmosphere and under the enforced expectation of death, he might well have died.

It so happened that about that time I was reading Howard Somervell's *After Everest*, a book describing his experiences as a mountaineer and medical missionary in India. Here he told the story of a schoolmaster at one of the Mission Boys' Schools who was suffering from a tubercular infection of the bone of the leg. Eventually the conclusion was reached that the only thing to do was to amputate the leg to save the young man's life. But the patient had other ideas. 'Will you give me three weeks? I want to try the effect of praying about it.' It was agreed that he might have that time, and on the next day he left for his home. In three weeks, true to his promise, he turned up. He had left the hospital feverish, ill and capable only of being carried about. He returned by car, but hobbling with a stick and looking much better. Although not completely healed the leg was much improved.

The medical people were amazed. What had he done to make so great an improvement? He said quite simply that he was sure that it was not the will of God that he should lose his leg and that he had before him a life of service to God if only he could keep both his leg and his life. So he called his family and friends together and asked them to unite in prayer that his leg might be completely healed. For a week a continuous chain of prayer was kept up by that family and his condition steadily improved. He went away again and came back three weeks later. The leg was now healed and he was able to walk upon it a little. A few months later, Somervell records, that young man was back at school, perfectly well and playing football with the boys. His comment was: 'This man, from a family which a few generations ago was worshipping devils, and despised as untouchable by the official religion of India, was able to exercise a faith in prayer which we so-called civilised Westerners have forgotten how to use.'[1]

In my youthful way, I put together these two stories of Indians who were facing illness. One felt himself surrounded by a malevolent force of evil and the other knew himself to be held by the benevolent power of love and prayer. One almost died from quite a trivial illness and the other recovered from what was a life-threatening disease. There must be something here, I felt, that merited further examination. When, at the end of the War, I returned again to theological study, I began to take an interest in the relationship of the doctrine of the atonement to concepts of healing and salvation.

I was greatly indebted at that time to the writings of William Temple, who, over forty years ago, was responsible for founding the Churches' Council for Health and Healing, and to Leslie Weatherhead, whose book, *Psychology, Religion, and Healing*, was a landmark in its time. Both these churchmen seemed to be affirming that the ministry of healing is firmly based in Christian Scripture and that the Church would neglect this aspect of ministry only at its peril.

Until recently the Church in our time has largely neglected the ministry of healing and assumed that God's power to heal, except within very prescribed limits, has been withdrawn from his Church. That there are problems in relation to this ministry, problems both psychological and theological, no one who is involved in it would deny. Some significant work has been done by scholars like the Blumhardts, father and son, D. S. Cairns and Morton Kelsey, and by the World Council of Churches' Christian Medical Commission, but on the whole the neglect of this field of study by theologians has been enormous. It may be that, with the quickening of interest in this ministry in all our churches and new developments in scientific understanding of matter, encouragement may be given to further theological enquiry and to a new dialogue between religion and medicine.

FACTORS WHICH HAVE LED TO RECOVERY

I see these principally in the following terms:

(i) An emerging holistic world view

Set over against the context of division between East and West, North and South, and the distinctively social factors that make for brokenness and alienation in society, there is also an emerging sense of change and transformation in our view of ourselves, our society and our world. In a BBC *Start the Week* programme in January 1989, Professor J. K. Galbraith referred to the recent growing understanding between the USA and the USSR and used a phrase which seemed to me to be significant. He spoke of 'deeper forces bringing them together'. These forces seem to be encouraging an urgent recognition of the need to live together as a human family if we are not to die together in a confrontational and competitive way.

The word 'holism' was coined by Jan Smuts in 1926 to describe 'the tendency of nature to produce wholes from the disordered grouping of units'. But the word actually reflects a much more ancient and eastern view of thought and is clearly seen in the Hebraic tradition. In medical terms holism has come to be used to explain the need for those who treat patients to see them as whole persons, body, mind and spirit, and to see them against an affecting environment – in short to see them as people and not as a collection of symptoms. The British Holistic Medical Association, set up in 1983, was an endeavour by doctors to further this holistic approach in medical practice. For it was clearly seen that the analytical method, though it had had great success and brought remarkable discoveries, could not deal completely with such a complex being as the human person.

(ii) The charismatic movement

Whatever else the charismatic movement has done for the churches in our time, it has encouraged people to be more expectant of God, more open to the power of the Holy Spirit and to one another. All this has quickened a new and prayerful interest in the healing ministry of the Church. The churches of charismatic renewal have done much to foster and further this ministry.

(iii) *The growth of complementary/alternative medicine*

With the increasing pressure on the National Health Service and the obvious limits to what can be provided by hard-pressed medical practitioners, there has been a growth of interest in alternative forms of therapy: homeopathy, herbalism, acupuncture, osteopathy and so on. The attraction of these forms of alternative medicine for many is that they are in the main holistic. They regard human beings as more than the sum of their parts and, as in the best of orthodox medicine, are concerned to cure people rather than diseases. A further reason for growth in this field is the recognition that medical resources are finite and a growing suspicion that some forms of treatment are less than beneficial. The over-reliance on drug therapy until nature seems to become retaliatory, an increasing range of drugs which prove to be harmful, and the growth of diseases actually caused by medical intervention, have all contributed to the search for alternative forms of treatment. The Church's ministry of healing, however, should not be thought of as another form of complementary medicine.

(iv) *Personal responsibility*

All this has led to a recognition that there are some things that we must do for ourselves, that we are responsible, that we are self-healing or disease-inducing agents. We now recognise that much illness is caused by the consumption of unhealthy or unsuitable foods. There are also those illnesses which arise from over-indulgence and false choices in consumption. As a migraine sufferer, I know the peril of taking too much cheese, chocolate or red wine. I also recognise the human tendency to try to restore the balance by corrective drugs which relieve the early signs and symptoms of such sickness but do not get to the root cause. We now know that drink, drugs, smoking and lack of proper exercise all take their toll. So we understand that a healthy and sensible life-style is important to true well-being.

(v) A recognition of what it means to be human

There is today increasing recognition that we are physical, mental, spiritual and *social* beings; that relationships matter, and relationships at every level: God, life, and the whole of creation, the earth beneath, the sky above, the air we breathe. Then there are the more personal relationships with members of our family and community groups. It is not until there is a breakdown of relationships at one or other of these structural levels that we recognise just how vulnerable we are, how important such relationships are to us and how much we need some kind of reconciliation, redemption and healing. All this leads us to see that disease is never simple; it is always more than it seems and involves the whole of life. To be human and to be healthy is to be able to see things in their unity and relatedness – this includes the unity, the relatedness of body, mind and spirit and involves a whole series of interlocking attitudes and relationships, not least our relationship with God and all that flows from him. Health, then, is essentially dynamic – not so much a destination as a way of travelling and much depends upon the company we keep and the quality of the relationships we enjoy.

THE CHURCHES' HEALING MINISTRY TODAY

It is not easy to get a complete picture. On the one hand, there is the reserve shown by many hierarchical figures and ecclesiastical bodies to anything which gives the impression of becoming a kind of religious band-waggon. On the other hand, there is steady growth in the number of churches which are taking seriously the healing ministry. Churches which ten years ago would never have considered services for healing now have 'laying-on-of-hands' as a regular part of the liturgy. This is not just in those churches that are influenced by charismatic renewal but also in those of a more conservative and liberal tradition. One can understand the reserve there is in some quarters about this, whilst at the same time wishing for rather less fence-sitting by those in high places. Undoubtedly there are distortions in the healing ministry and there is always the possibility that without due thought and proper control the healing ministry can lead to malpractice and an appeal to magic.

One such instance I remember with disturbing clarity. We were having a family celebration in London which included a visit to the theatre. In the interval we gathered in the bar. Our conversation was interrupted by a young woman falling in a faint at my feet. My elder son and I carried the limp form out of the smoke-filled bar and into a quiet corridor where there was a little fresh air. We stayed with her in the hope that she would soon be revived. As we waited, a woman came past the end of the corridor, took in the situation in a flash and then, whilst keeping her distance, lifted her right hand majestically and pronounced, 'I'm a healer. In the name of the Father, Son and Holy Spirit, be healed.' Directing her attention to me, she said, 'She'll be all right now.' She then turned on her heel and went back for the second half of the show, leaving us with the body! I'm pleased to say that the young lady very soon recovered. Whether this was a result of the healer's intervention we shall never know. In my estimation the incident was enough to put the healing ministry back ten years. There was no personal involvement, no continuing concern, but just a rather lordly pronouncement. The good lady may have thought that she was continuing the New Testament tradition. In my book her approach smacked too much of an uncostly 'zapping'.

There are many who are rightly anxious about certain practitioners in the field of healing. This anxiety may be caused by a recognition that Christ is not central to the ministry or because some practices seem to have less to do with faith, in the sense of being open and receptive to God, than with manipulative suggestion and even sometimes mass hysteria.

It was during the 1950s that I first developed major reservations about healing rallies which took place outside the normal life of the church. This was partly because the emphasis was not always sufficiently Christ-centred, but also because I felt that people were often being manipulated and encouraged to believe in magic. I also wondered about pastoral follow-up and whether the latter state of those being healed might not on occasion be worse than the former.

At a service in Manchester, I saw some remarkable 'healings' by the Spiritualist, the late Harry Edwards. One woman with one leg shorter than the other was asked to take off the built-up boot she was wearing and, after ministry, she walked perfectly well down the church aisle with no shoes on. The leg had been healed. But some weeks later, one of the tabloid newspapers carried the story of the miraculous healing and went on to tell how the young woman was still wearing her sister's shoes because she was afraid that if she bought new shoes her leg might suddenly 'shrink' again. Was that, one asked, a true healing?

I recently took part in a conference for directors of residential homes and day centres for healing. One session provided a careful delineation of two very different approaches to the healing ministry, one in the North of England and one in the South. The director of the latter was quietly impressive as he spoke of the development of their work over many years. It is a centre rich in traditional Anglican worship and churchmanship. What was described was a ministry of Word and Sacrament, all done decently and in good order, and from which the healing gently flows. There were some wise things said about the need for a true theology and a right expectation of healing.

The other home was in the North of England and one which had recently been featured in the television *Encounter* programme called 'Who needs the Devil?' As the story unfolded, we marvelled at the faith, hope and courage which had marked the development of this new healing centre. There was so much that was admirable about the work that was being done there. Every effort was being made by those running the centre to stand alongside those who were ill and also act as a resource centre for the local churches. We have all seen the dangers of too individualistic styles of ministry resting on the gifts and authority of a single person. It was, therefore, good to be assured that the centre depends heavily on team-work and the help of associate counsellors. We were also told that the ministry is confrontational and directive and that something like forty per cent of those who come require, and are offered, deliverance ministry. Many would feel that this is a remarkably high percentage and it does make one ask whether the Pendle witches are even more active today than formerly, or whether a form of belief is being imposed upon the visitors which might not have been present otherwise.

I hope I shall be forgiven for singling out these two particular homes. It does seem that they represent two wings of the Christian healing movement in Britain today which are, each in their own way, significant and influential.

It is good to see a recovery of the healing ministry within the local church. Many churches now have regular times set apart for such a service. Many have discovered that not only has their liturgy been given a new dimension but that there has been a growth in spirituality within the congregation. They have also discovered that 'signs and wonders' are not only within the gift of visiting evangelists but do occur quietly and excitingly within the life of an obedient and faithful Christian community today.

There are sadly some who will turn to the healing ministry because other forms of ministry seem to have failed. It is as if they are saying, 'We have tried missions and they have brought little by way of results; we have been concerned with social welfare but others do that better than we can; we have become involved in political issues but that only caused trouble in the congregation; let us try spiritual healing; that seems to be the thing for today.' That we have been unsuccessful in other branches of outreach is not an adequate motive for including healing in our church programme. Indeed, even to put it that way seems to suggest a basic misunderstanding of what a healing ministry is all about. It can never be at its best when seen as an optional extra but must be an integral part of a total ministry.

A useful illustration of the way in which the danger of separateness can be avoided and a total ministry exercised may be seen at St Marylebone Parish Church, London. There the normal activities of a parish church are regularly pursued. What is different is that the crypt, which once served as a burial chamber, is now converted into a healing and counselling centre, where music therapy, a NHS medical practice, counselling and Christian ministry together serve the needs not just of the local congregation but of the whole community. The fulfilment of this vision of an Anglican priest, Revd Christopher Hamel Cooke, and his colleagues is a working model of what the Church should be doing in the sphere of health and healing. They would be the first to admit that there is a long way to go before they are satisfied that the vision is completely fulfilled. A start has been made, however, and it is for others to work out in their own way belief in the fundamental principle enunciated so clearly by the Anglican Report on Healing at Lambeth, 1930, 'that the power to exercise spiritual healing is taught by Christ to be the natural heritage of Christian people who are living in fellowship with God, and is part of the ministry of Christ through His Body the Church.'[2]

A completely different model of health centre was established in Balsall Heath, Birmingham, in 1977, based on the writings of Dr Bob Lambourne. There Dr Anthony Bird set up an experimental group practice in co-operation with Queen's Theological College, the University of Birmingham Department of Theology and the Christian Medical Commission of the World Council of Churches. In an area where the bulk of the population were Asian, a primary health care unit was established in the inner city. Dr Malcolm Rigler first pioneered this experimental practice. It was the first in Britain to explore the role of the nurse practitioner. When Dr Rigler left, Dr Anthony Bird gave up his work as Principal of Queen's to resume general practice in the centre.[3]

Overall, it seems, there is still a need for the Church to come to terms with that resolution of the Lambeth Conference of 1930, which was reaffirmed in 1978. There is also pressing need for more careful teaching about, and training in, the healing ministry in our churches, theological colleges, ordination and post-ordination courses. We are here involved in very sensitive issues and without proper teaching and training our best endeavours can go sadly awry.

SIGNS OF A RESPONSIBLE APPROACH

As the modern movement in the Church's ministry of healing grows, so it becomes necessary to ensure that what can be something of a minefield is preserved as a 'many splendour'd thing'. We require perhaps some standards of judgement, some criteria of what is and is not acceptable. Medical people might speak of validation. I would suggest that four criteria might be usefully applied.

(i) Due respect should be given to people as children of God. This means that they should not be used or manipulated for our own advantage, or to prove a point, or even for what we might deem to be their own good. One way of watching that is continually to remind ourselves that true healing is always a gift of God. It should, therefore, be seen as a fundamental part of the Church's ministry (not our own). This has implications in terms of correction and continuing oversight of this ministry by the Church.

(ii) It is vitally important to be able to see medicine as an ally and to recognise that there are many pathways to healing. The illustrations of St Marylebone and Balsall Heath are just two of the places in which the insights of religion and medicine are being brought together in a creative manner in Britain. Work done by the Christian Medical Commission of the W.C.C. indicate that many of the countries in Africa and Asia are further down this particular road than we are. We still need to hear that word of A. Graham Ikin:

> A cup of cold water may save a life, a pint of blood given for transfusion may save another, an injection of penicillin may save a third, and the love and faith of someone who has learned through prayer how to provide a link between a sufferer and the 'life more abundant' . . . may save others.[4]

The Churches' Council for Health and Healing, in conjunction with the Royal College of General Practitioners, has recently published the report of a joint working party to explore ways in which they could work together in providing care for people. It aims to provide a Christian perspective on whole-person medicine as it affects both the church and medicine today. It urges closer co-operation between general practitioners and ministers of religion and greater sharing between medical and theological students. We do need to learn to acknowledge the contribution that each can bring to human well-being and to try to work more closely together.

(iii) In order to avoid the dangers of extreme individualism and distortion which can arise in personal ministry, it is important to keep in mind the corporate aspects of healing. That is why the Christian healing ministry should be firmly anchored in the life of the church community. It should find its expression not only in special services for healing but also in the Communion service, the mid-week meeting for prayer, and perhaps in the church luncheon club. We should never forget that the goal of historic Judaism, out of which Christianity came, was always collective redemption: shalom, a state of total well-being, of being right with God and with one's neighbour, indeed with the whole environment. Christianity at its best carries the same emphasis. It is all things in heaven and on earth that are to be reconciled to God through his son Jesus Christ.

(iv) The fourth sign of a responsible approach to Christian healing ministry is a readiness to see beyond the physical, and to see healing involving something more than cure. Healing in the sense of cure, for the Christian, is always secondary to a true faith in, and relationship with, the God and Father of our Lord Jesus Christ. I suspect sometimes that there is a kind of idolatry of health in the rich countries of the world. I am not too sure just how healthy this is. It encourages us to make false judgements about both divinity and humanity. It leads us sometimes to take a superficial view of suffering and a distorted attitude to those who suffer. Some time ago the actor Esmond Knight was asked if his blindness was a handicap to him in his profession. He said that it was, in various ways. The most painful, however, was the fact that when fellow actors saw him sitting in the green-room having a cup of tea, they would not join him but would walk to the other end of the room.

This same idolatry blinds us to the fact that the ultimate judgement of our response to suffering lies in its quality rather than its success. It also encourages the heresy put out by some enthusiasts for spiritual healing that only lack of faith and hope in God stand between the sufferer and healing. This attitude often leads to considerable problems for the sick and those who care for them. We do well to remember that wholeness in the biblical sense does not mean a perfection to be achieved here and now, but rather the achievement of a relationship with God that enables us to transcend limitations and transform relationships. It involves the rejection of any idealistic model of health based upon the idea of a perfect organism – what might be called the 'Greek vase syndrome' – something perfect in shape and form.

Biblical wholeness is not of form but of action, direction and purpose. The disciples of Jesus Christ should know that all too well. The torn flesh and gaping wounds seen on Calvary should help us to dispose of any view of wholeness that consists of perfection of shape and form. But then, the gospel assures us, the agony and anguish having reached their peak, Jesus placed himself unreservedly in the hands of God: 'Father, into thy hands I commit my spirit.'[5] This was fulfilment, a complete understanding of what reality is and who he was. This was healing of a kind that alone has eternal meaning.

2

Healing in the Biblical Tradition

At a conference in Port of Spain, Trinidad, on the churches' role in health and wholeness, Professor William Watty told how John Wesley ventured into the practice of medicine.[1] In a letter to a friend, Wesley explained that when doing his rounds, he discovered that many of his followers were chronically ill, partly because there was no remedy readily available, partly because they were so poor they could not afford what had been prescribed for them. Wesley, it seems, had spent some twenty or more years studying 'anatomy and physic' and had taken an apothecary and a surgeon to assist him, determining 'not to go out of my depth, but to leave all difficult and complicated cases to such physicians as the patients should choose'.

One day a certain William Kirkham presented himself with a very bad cough. Wesley asked, 'How long have you had it?' The man replied, 'About three score years. It began when I was eleven years old.' Wesley confessed, 'I was nothing glad that this man should come first, fearing our not curing him might discourage the others. However, I looked up to God and said, "Take this three or four times a day. If it does you no good, it will do you no harm." ' Wesley records, 'He took it two or three days. His cough was cured and he has not returned to this day.'

'Now,' said Wesley, 'let candid men judge, does humility require me to deny this notorious fact? To say I by my own skill restored this man to health, or God did it by his own almighty power?' William Watty, in recounting this story, posed two further questions, 'Was the man cured because for the first time someone cared enough to give him something for his cough? Was the cough he had endured for sixty years a physical affliction or the affliction of an aching soul?'

William Watty then went on to suggest: 'Wesley shows us how close the world of the eighteenth century was to the world of the Bible and how remote we are in the twentieth century from both.' Certainly Wesley stood very clearly in the biblical tradition which saw that the soul cannot be separated from the body. One of the basic concepts in the Bible is that of solidarity. God is related to the world as the soul is related to the body. Health is personal well-being, in terms of harmony between soul and body, social harmony, in terms of right relationships with others and the ability to walk humbly with God.

Moreover, as God is the source of all creation and the giver of all life, so he is the source of all power, including the power that causes miracles to happen. To those of us caught up in the grip of a secular tradition and suffering the effects of a reductionist faith, it is perhaps salutary to be recalled to the biblical tradition in which our faith is grounded.

Our difficulty may well lie in knowing just how to bridge the gap between the world of Wesley, or the world of the Bible, and our modern world. One way is simply to assert, or to assume, that there is no difference and to refuse any concession to modern thought or current experience. That way lies biblical conservatism and stern anti-reductionism – a tempting alternative in a day of psychological and ecological insecurity. No one who is aware of developments in modern churchmanship in the West can underestimate its power.

Another way is to close our minds to biblical insights and become locked into what is increasingly becoming an outdated reductionism, which holds little promise of satisfying any deeper experiences of the religious life or of providing the power to develop it. Could it be, as some suggest, that the expansion both of scientific horizons and of religious awareness, developing contemporaneously, may lead to a new kind of convergence which heralds a fresh appreciation of biblical tradition and a new era of human consciousness? The prophets of true insight, with the mystics, have surely always known that the inward journey and the outward journey are one – that the scientific and the spiritual must march together if we are to be whole. Any alternative is bound to issue in dissonance and disintegration.

Having said that, we still have to allow that what we are talking about is a book that stretches over one thousand years in writing. There is great value in trying to see it all in a panoramic view, looking at broad trends and a gradual development in the Hebrew view of God.

HEALING IN THE OLD TESTAMENT

If we are to understand the Old Testament, we have to recognise that there is nothing monochrome about its view of God and his purposes, just as there is nothing very tidy about its presentation of the problems of sickness and health. Whilst there are strong lines of consistent thought about the nature of God, there is an engaging readiness to allow God certain freedom in regard to his practices.

The first thing that the Old Testament says about God is that he is the author of creation, and the essential characteristic of that creation is that it is good. 'And God saw everything that he had made, and behold, it was very good.'[2] This pattern of essential harmony was broken by the human thrust for knowledge of good and evil. Whilst it is possible to misinterpret the nature of that breach, it is impossible to underestimate its significance. The primal dream of harmony with the environment was shattered by human disobedience. This was met by judgement and promise. Judgement is the immediate response to disobedience. The promise is restoration and renewal when the appropriate response is made. Meanwhile, according to the 'Deuteronomic view':

> It is I who deal death and life;
> when I have struck, it is I who heal
> (and none can deliver from my hand).[3]

Sickness here was seen largely as God's rebuke for sin. There was no limit to the difficulties and disasters that Yahweh could conjure up for those who were disobedient. The plagues which the Egyptians suffered for their hardness of heart in refusing to allow Moses and his people to go free included physical illness and ended up with the death of their first-born.

What Karl Barth describes as 'the divine Magna Carta' in the matter of health and healing is God's great promise to Israel:

> If you will diligently hearken to the voice of the Lord your God, and do that which is right in his eyes, and give heed to his commandments and keep all his statutes, I will put none of the diseases upon you which I put upon the Egyptians; for I am the Lord, your healer.[4]

Sickness, then, according to this fairly dominant tradition, represented a breakdown of relationship between God and his people. It is this tradition which is being followed when we think of sickness as flowing from the Fall.

Behind this tradition lies, first of all, the Hebrew view of solidarity: 'For as in Adam all die . . .'. The sin of one affects the whole community. So David's sin had its effect upon all the people. The other factor is the Hebrews' firm sense of monotheism which made them reject any idea of sickness and suffering deriving from the demonic power of various gods or evil spirits. Yahweh, unlike the multitudinous gods of the Egyptians or Babylonians, was one God and was therefore the source of good and evil, sickness as well as health. It was later in post-exilic times that foreign ideas and influences began to infiltrate into Hebrew thinking.

But there is another strand in the Old Testament experience which, whilst it does not have the centrality of the other view, is not to be ignored. It is expressed in certain healing stories, in some of the Psalms, in certain passages of Isaiah and, above all, in the great protest of Job. It is this line which Jesus follows in his teaching and ministry.

We have the basic assurance that God can heal and some eloquent testimonies to this truth. We see women like Sarah healed of their infertility.[5] We have moving stories of Elijah and Elisha healing a child.[6] We have Elisha cleansing Naaman of his leprosy and see that no sin was attributed to the sick

man.[7] We also have the suggestion that there are alien forces
at work in the world which are opposed to God and his goodness, and these are themselves in part responsible for many of
the trials and tribulations to which we are subject.

The most eloquent protest against the Deuteronomic, or
legalist, theory of sickness and suffering comes in the story of
Job. Indeed, one of the main purposes of that book is to
challenge the theory that sickness and suffering are causally
related to sin and disobedience to God. Job was a righteous
man, surely one of God's favourites. He feared God and turned
away from all evil. Yahweh said to Satan: 'Have you considered
my servant Job, that there is none like him on the earth, a
blameless and upright man, who fears God and turns away
from evil?'[8] But Satan will have none of this. 'Does Job fear
God for nought?' In other words, 'Do you think this is all
disinterested goodness? Is it not that you have protected him
and his family and that he knows which side his bread is but-
tered on? If you just touch him where it hurts, he'll soon change
his tune!'

So Job was really taken apart. Not just his cattle and servants
but also his sons and daughters were killed. Yet his reaction,
from the Hebrew point of view, was the ideal one. He arose,
rent his robe, shaved his head and fell on the ground and
worshipped, saying: 'Naked I came from my mother's womb,
and naked shall I return; the Lord gave, and the Lord has
taken away; blessed be the name of the Lord' (1:21). Here is
a picture of a healthy man in adversity. He makes the correct
response. He knows what is required of him. But Satan hasn't
finished with him yet! 'Touch his bone and his flesh, and he
will curse thee to thy face.' In spite of continuing adversity,
the taunts of his wife and the far from helpful counsel of his
friends, Job maintains his faith in God (with just a hint of the
occasional rather human 'wobbly'). 'Shall we receive good at
the hand of God, and shall we not receive evil?' In the end
Job finds healing in a new and vivid experience of God. The
intellectual problems remain unanswered but pain and deprivation have lost their power to destroy him. The whole book
is a profound discussion of the problem of unmerited suffering.
Throughout we find the writers trying to maintain the legalistic

theory of the origin of suffering, but they are never finally able to prevent this other strand coming through. It was this strand that was taken up by Jesus who related sickness, at least in part, to the influence of evil spirits rather than coming directly from God, and therefore meriting our compassion and practical help.

The other factor which deserves consideration is the Hebrew view of the person. The Bible declares that we are made in the image of God. We are given our place as God's agents to act as estate-managers over Creation. It is a heavy responsibility made even more grave by the fact that we alone of all created things can accept or deny God, hamper or fulfil his purposes.

A second thing that the Old Testament makes plain is that the human being is, in Wheeler Robinson's phrase, 'an animated body, not an incarnated soul'. In line with the general concepts of solidarity and corporateness, there was not the tendency to separate body and soul that there is today. There was instead a marked sense of the unity of human personality. The body was the whole being, at its best enlivened and empowered by the Spirit of God.

The Old Testament gave emphasis to the corporate nature of salvation. It is sometimes difficult for us in twentieth-century western society to recognise just how much in biblical times salvation/healing was seen in terms of community, rather than in individual terms. Israel is a people under a corporate covenant with God. This means that the individual does not stand alone; when one member suffers, the whole community shares in that suffering. When one member sins, the whole community is affected. Salvation for the Hebrew was something that would be realised in the coming of the Messiah in whom, and by whom, the 'wholeness' of the community would be perfected and its unity restored. The Hebrew word *shalom*, commonly translated 'peace', gives a hint of the same concept. It includes the idea of 'welfare' or 'well-being' but goes beyond the individual experience of that. It suggests fulfilment, community with others, lasting well-being. It involves justice, self-discipline and responsible freedom. Shalom was to be the conspicuous blessing of the messianic kingdom. It signified a new and settled relationship between God and his people. So it described the happiness which people enjoy when they have a good relationship with God and one another. The Chief Rabbi, Sir Immanuel Jakobvits, in a recent radio broadcast, described shalom as 'two houses side by side; happiness within the households and peace between them'.

Another significant strand in the Old Testament view of the person is that we are to be God's agents in creation and re-creation. Throughout we are reminded that the agents of salvation/healing are ordinary people who often did extraordinary things: Moses leading his people out of captivity in Egypt, the Psalmist crying for deliverance, the prophets calling God's people to walk in God's ways. The promise is that when this response has been truly made, then the blind shall see, the deaf hear, the lame walk and the 'tongue of the dumb sing for joy' (Isaiah 35:5–6).

In summary, one can say that there are four elements in the Old Testament view of healing:

(i) God is the author of healing; he is personal, active and a living Lord, the source of all power, including the power to work miracles.

(ii) His intervention is usually through the mediation of another. Remember how Naaman's healing was by an unknown servant girl. This carries with it the implication of human responsibility as co-workers with God.

(iii) There is a strong sense of corporate solidarity both in sickness and in health. We cannot evade our personal responsibility for the health and well-being of society.

(iv) There is a clear understanding that healing involves the restoration of true and harmonious relationships.

If one were looking for a single sentence to summarise the Old Testament teaching on health and healing and to provide a link with New Testament thought, it would be difficult to find anything more appropriate than that word of Hans Küng: 'God's Kingdom is creation healed'.[9]

HEALING IN THE NEW TESTAMENT

Mark characterises the ministry of Jesus as being a threefold one of preaching, teaching and healing. I suppose it was not until I heard the actor, Alex McCowen, reciting the Gospel of Mark in a stage performance in London that I fully realised just how much of that Gospel is given up to Jesus' healing ministry. Some twenty per cent of Mark's Gospel is devoted to this. Matthew and Luke use respectively nine and eight per cent of their material for this purpose. John uses five per cent.

Jesus' commission to the Twelve is recorded by Matthew:

> And preach as you go, saying, 'The kingdom of heaven is at hand.' Heal the sick, raise the dead, cleanse lepers, cast out demons. You received without pay, give without pay.[10]

The healings of Jesus, far from conflicting with his preaching, were the signs which lent truth and reality to his words. They were an extension of his concern and compassion for people. On another level they represented the breaking in of the Kingdom of God into a situation of disability, disease and distress. In answer to the charge that he was a sorcerer, Jesus replied:

> And if I cast out demons by Be-elzebul, by whom do your sons cast them out? Therefore they shall be your judges. But if it is by the Spirit of God that I cast out demons, then the kingdom of God has come upon you.[11]

When the disciples of John came to inquire whether Jesus was the expected Messiah, or should they continue looking for another, Jesus replied in terms recalling Isaiah 35:5 and 61:1:

> Go and tell John what you hear and see: the blind receive their sight and the lame walk, lepers are cleansed and the deaf hear, and the dead are raised up, and the poor have good news preached to them. And blessed is he who takes no offense at me.[12]

In this way the healing works were the 'signs' of the preaching of the Kingdom. People will either accept the signs and believe in him or refuse the signs and reject him.

It is important to remember that in Jesus' day all healing was seen as an activity in which spiritual powers were involved. It might be the physical healing of the sick man at the pool of Bethesda or the sending away of the seven devils from Mary Magdalene or the curing of Zacchaeus of his grasping attitude to life. Each of these situations, different in kind as they might seem to us, were to be seen as part of God's victory over everything which distorts and binds his creation. So Jesus' power is seen as being set against the demonic powers affecting every part of our life in this world: the burden of disease, the curse of occult powers or the bondage of sin and guilt. He is the one anointed

> to proclaim release to the captives
> and recovering of sight to the blind,
> to set at liberty those who are oppressed,
> to proclaim the acceptable year of the Lord.[13]

His mission was to bring the healing power of God's love to bear upon the moral, mental and spiritual sickness of his time. It was a question of rescuing people from a situation in which they seemed powerless to help themselves. Jesus knew and disclosed that new power, the power of God's love, to bring them from the pit of brokenness and sin.

The methods he used varied considerably. Sometimes he simply called upon the faith of the individual seeking healing.[14] Sometimes he called upon the faith of those around the sick person.[15] Sometimes he used touch alone, as in Nazareth when he was hindered by unbelief.[16] Sometimes he used touch along with some kind of anointing.[17]

In the raising of Lazarus, the healing of the ten lepers, the freeing of the Gerasene demoniac, the healing of the nobleman's son at a distance and the paralysed man at the pool of Bethesda, there was the use of speech and command.[18] Sometimes Jesus used both speech and touch together. Almost half the examples of healing in the Gospels are characterised by this approach. Whatever methods were used, there was always a strongly sacramental element. Both word and touch were used as bearers and signs of God's healing love and power. This may be seen in relation to three healing stories in the Gospels.

(i) The healing at Bethesda (John 5:1–9)

The restoration of the impotent man at the pool of Bethesda is a fascinating account of a man healed by word alone. Jesus asked the man who had been lame for thirty-eight years, 'Do you want to be healed?' This might seem to be a curious question under the circumstances. But most of us have known people who appear to discover the meaning of life in and through their sickness; their need for attention is greater than their need for health. This man might have discovered certain compensations in this strange beggar-life in the shadows of the pool of Bethesda.

The lame man's response to Jesus indicated that here was one who really did want to be made whole. Jesus went on to tell him what to do about it: 'Rise, take up your pallet, and walk.' The man was healed instantly and did as Jesus commanded. The next time we meet this once-lame man is in the temple. Jesus saw him and said to him: 'See, you are well! Sin no more, that nothing worse befall you.' The suggestion here is that the patient's illness followed from a distorted response to life. This may not have been a conscious reaction but one which, unless it was changed, could lead to a renewal and escalation of the sickness. The man went away and told the Jews who had healed him. All this indicates that there is more than one stage in healing of this kind. There is first the desire, the overwhelming desire to be healed. Secondly, there must be the act of commitment by which we express our readiness to accept in faith the gift that God offers to us. The final stage is that of being ready to acknowledge before God and others all that he has done for us. I remember reading of an African who had been spectacularly healed of yaws by penicillin. When the doctor called the following day, the whole family was caught up in uproarious deep belly laughter, including the patient. 'God is good, God is good, God is good', they cried continually in a spirit of praise. When we lose that kind of response to

God's goodness, we become impoverished and diminished as human beings.

(ii) The healing of the deaf-mute (Mark 7:31–7)

Here was a man who was deaf and had difficulty with his speech. The RSV suggests he had 'an impediment in his speech'. He may not have been deaf all his life, and his speech defect may have grown with his increasing deafness. Taking the man aside, Jesus put his fingers into the man's ears and touched his tongue with spittle. Then looking up to heaven he said: 'Eph'phatha', that is, 'Be opened'. The man began to hear, 'his tongue was released and he spoke plainly'. Jesus charged the people to tell no one, but with typical human contrariness they went out to proclaim the miracle more fully, saying: 'He has done all things well; he even makes the deaf hear and the dumb speak.'

The story is a fascinating one, not only because it fits readily into what might be called popular healing stories, but because it has certain parallels with pagan healing stories in its use of sacramental acts and vivid, dramatic words. The fundamental difference between this story and other stories from pagan literature is that Jesus' healings are understood as manifestations of his messianic authority and signs of the coming Kingdom. When Jesus heals, he anticipates, and in some sense inaugurates, the Kingdom. He affirms hope, not only for a deaf man with a speech defect, but for the whole world.

(iii) The man blind from birth (John 9)

In many ways this is a key passage for an understanding of the biblical doctrine of healing. It tells the story of a man who had been blind from birth. The disciples, following much Jewish thought of the time, asked, 'Master, who sinned, this man or his parents, that he was born blind?' Jesus refused to accept that sin and suffering are necessarily causally related. In any case he was not in the business of attributing blame. Anyone looking for an easy answer to the problem of suffering in terms of moral fault is likely to have a hard time with this story. In his reply, Jesus changes the whole direction of the discussion.

'It was not that this man sinned, or his parents, but that the works of God might be made manifest in him.'

Jesus was not saying that the man had been born blind, or even brought before him at that time, in order that he might be the means of furthering the preaching or publicity of the gospel. What the passage is essentially about is the battle between light and darkness. One of the works of God is to bring light where there is darkness. Until the true light comes, all people are in darkness. This man is simply a representative of the whole human race. Part of our condition is that we live mostly in the darkness, that we are blind to the truth of God. Lesslie Newbigin has said: 'The distinction is not between those who are blind and those who see; it is between those who know they are blind and those who think that they see.'[19] Jesus' particular quarrel here was with those who, instead of entering into the situation with healing aid, were prepared to stand on the sidelines, suggesting explanations and imputing blame. A true theology in this instance would not be unduly concerned with explanations, but with trying to understand how the healing power of God could be brought into this situation to effect change and renewal.

The method used by Jesus here suggests links with miraculous healings in the Hellenistic world, where the saliva of a saintly or exalted person was seen as possessing healing properties. John Marsh sees in the mingling of clay and spittle an allusion to the creation of man out of the dust of the ground.[20] This, with the instruction to go and wash in the pool of Siloam, indicates that Jesus is not concerned solely with restoration of function but with effecting a re-creation and regeneration of the whole person. The means may be simple; the implications, as this story indicates, may be staggering. The Gospel tells how the crowds rejected the man who had been healed but Jesus found him and asked whether he believed in the Son of man. For a moment he faltered, wondering who this might be. Then, when Jesus revealed himself, he said, 'Lord, I believe', and worshipped him.

Jesus' way was, wherever possible, to bring people into a new relationship with God by the various methods of touching, seeking, speaking commands, by compassion and assurance of forgiveness, so that the power of God might break through to them and restore them. He also demonstrated that whilst sickness can be caused by sin, there is no reason for supposing this will always be the case. He specifically rejected the theory that all that afflicts us is caused by sin. Speaking about the Galileans whose blood Pilate had mingled with their sacrifice, Jesus said:

> Do you think that these Galileans were worse sinners than all the other Galileans, because they suffered thus? I tell you, No; but unless you repent you will all likewise perish. Or those eighteen upon whom the tower in Siloam fell and killed them, do you think that they were worse offenders than all the others who dwelt in Jerusalem? I tell you, No; but unless you repent you will all likewise perish.[21]

We often make the assumption that there can only be one centre to a person's being. So each person is in control of self and so able to determine action by conscious choice. Jesus, however, saw that it is more complicated than this – that there can be more than one centre and various ways of orientation or disorientation. Sickness, in Jesus' time, was often attributed to a primary force of evil in the world. He believed that human beings were often under the baneful influence of this power, or powers, which are hostile to God. It may well be that sin does leave one more open to the invasion of these hostile forces. The person who is empty of God, without spiritual defences, is much more likely to be subject to the power of such forces.[22] Hence the call to repentance. For this is the way by which we are enabled to give hospitality to the Spirit of God – the power that defeats all other powers and brings unity where before there had been division. But Jesus did not inquire whether a person was good or bad, whether repentance and renewal had taken place, before he ministered to them.

HEALING IN THE EARLY CHURCH

The Early Church obviously took seriously Jesus' commission to heal. In the Epistle of James we read:

Is any one among you suffering? Let him pray. Is any cheerful? Let him sing praise. Is any among you sick? Let him call for the elders of the church, and let them pray over him, anointing him with oil in the name of the Lord; and the prayer of faith will save the sick man, and the Lord will raise him up; and if he has committed sins, he will be forgiven.[23]

The passage suggests that prayer and praise are effectual remedies for a whole host of human disorders. We now know that faith and hope are life-giving, fear and despair are destructive. The prayer of faith says something to us about how little we expect of God. The anointing with oil reminds us of a custom long lost or misapplied. The injunction to call for the elders of the church to pray over the sick challenges us at the level of our church membership. There is also the less-than-appealing advice: 'Therefore confess your sins to one another, and pray for one another, that you may be healed.' Now we may be ready to pray for one another, but really, confessing our sins to one another is another thing entirely!

Dr Arnold Bittlinger tells the story of Helga, which provides a suitable challenge on this neglected area of spirituality.[24] Helga was suffering from advanced multiple sclerosis, in hospital and completely unable to move. The medical report indicated that the illness had become terminal. At this point Helga remembered once having read a verse in the Epistle of James which spoke of prayer for the sick. She asked a friend who was visiting her to find the verse in her New Testament. The friend leafed through the Epistle of James until she found the appropriate verses.

Nothing else had been of much use, so Helga decided to try out the advice in James. A message was sent to the elders of the congregation asking them to come and pray with her. One can just imagine the scene as the elders stood at that girl's bedside, feeling a mixture of compassion and personal embarrassment. So they read together the passage from James 5, then stopped, somewhat taken aback. The passage spoke not only of prayer but also of confession: 'Therefore confess your sins to one another, that you may be healed.' It looked as though the confession of sin was an essential preliminary to praying with the sick. A long silence fell and into this silence God began to speak, first in one person's life and then another. God spoke in this way to Helga too. Then one of the elders began to speak, telling the others what God had shown him, then another and another. Last of all, Helga too confessed her sins. Meanwhile something strange was happening in her room. It seemed as though it was filled with light and warmth, as though a new love had sprung up between those present.

The outcome of all this is that Helga was healed. She sat up, got out of bed, tried cautiously to take a few steps and then began to run along the corridor, up the stairs and back again. Bittlinger tells how this young woman is now healthy and happy, has trained as a nurse and now cares for multiple sclerosis patients whose suffering she can so fully share. We may feel that that is fine for Helga, but what about Maureen or Mary who do not receive that kind of healing? Indeed that is a real problem. I just wonder how many remain unhealed because we are not ready to open up ourselves to God and to one another, as those elders did at Helga's bedside.

We have to accept, of course, that physical healing does not always follow the prayer made in faith. We have the poignant story of Paul's thorn in the flesh to remind us of this:

> Three times I besought the Lord about this, that it should leave me; but he said to me, 'My grace is sufficient for you, for my power is made perfect in weakness.' I will all the more gladly boast of my weaknesses, that the power of Christ may rest upon me.[25]

All kinds of suggestions have been made as to what Paul meant by this metaphor. Was he referring to stammering, deafness, bodily injury, an infection of the eyes, migraine, epilepsy, malaria or what? Remember that Paul used the word 'flesh' to cover the whole person, body and soul. The important thing for Paul was that this experience of frailty and weakness was also a source of strength in that it was instrumental in leading to a great discovery – that God's grace was sufficient for all his needs.

Paul seems concerned to assure us, first of all, of God's

readiness to bring his own particular kind of healing; but also to underline the importance of response to any kind of crisis situation. 'Response' is a crucial word whether we are thinking of healing or salvation. Indeed the quality of the response we make to any sickness determines the character of the healing we enjoy. Health for the Christian means responding to life with all its trials and traumas, its liabilities and limitations in a mature way without losing our hold on God. Christians, whilst affirming and applauding the achievements of medicine, are primarily interested in a quality of life which is independent of wellness or illness – a life whose source and goal are union with God. Wellness or illness may make it easier to live such a Christian life-style, but neither wellness nor illness constitute a typically Christian style of life.

Equally, a healthy society is one in which the whole of society's life and experience is faced responsibly and together. So this word 'response' helps us to distinguish between healing and curing. It may also provide an understandable link between that total victory which Jesus accomplished by his death and resurrection and those other forms of healing which are open to us but are clearly anchored in human life. It is important, therefore, for us to see connections between what happens in our local hospitals and in our local churches, between the relationships of black and white in South Africa (or Birmingham, Brixton or Bristol) and Protestant and Catholic in Northern Ireland (or Liverpool or Glasgow). All these should be seen as the spheres in which our response to the love of God in Jesus Christ is placed under critical judgement. They also represent particular opportunities for development of the Church's ministry of healing.

This, in part, is how I interpret those words of Jesus on the night of the Last Supper: 'Truly, truly, I say to you, he who believes in me will also do the works that I do; and greater works than these will he do, because I go to the Father.'[26] Part of what Jesus meant here must surely relate to the proclamation of the Kingdom (in itself a ministry of healing); in due course the message of the Kingdom will be carried far beyond Jerusalem, Judaea and Samaria. But if preaching, teaching and healing go together, there are also those specific miracles of healing

seen in Jesus which will be repeated in the lives of his followers.
Remember how Paul in his lists of the gifts which came to the
Church included specifically the gift of healing.

That surely is not all that Jesus meant. One afternoon I
visited Papworth hospital and met a young woman who ten
days before had had a complete heart and lung transplant. She
was now walking in the hospital corridor – walking for the first
time for years without physical distress. I had to acknowledge
this, as the woman did, as a modern miracle. Is it too much to
recognise this as one of the 'greater works'? Surgeons with
their remarkable new techniques and physicians with their
wonder drugs today possess powers which to the ancient world
would seem miraculous and god-like.

It is not a great step from this to recognising that our
responsibility for the nature and ordering of society, which has
its genesis in the Old Testament prophetic tradition and its
confirmation in the teaching of Jesus, also has to be worked
out in our own day. We then have to keep a watchful eye on
what happens in political terms in regard to arms control, health
provision through the National Health Service, education in
our universities, schools and colleges, what happens to the
elderly, the young and unemployed, for all this can make or
mar the health of our society. So often the community needs
to be healed if individual sickness and suffering are not to be
compounded.

The Bible begins with a God who created the world in love.
It ends with a vision of the city of God, having the river of the
water of life flowing through it. On either side of the river was
the tree of life with its twelve kinds of fruit, yielding its fruit
each month, 'and the leaves of the tree were for the healing of
the nations'.[27] In this way we see that the God who was concerned about Creation, that it should be good, is also concerned
about re-creation, renewal and healing. The golden thread that
links the Old Testament to the New is the divine love for all
that he has made. It is this love, which operates at the heart
of life and operates for healing, which was seen in its perfection
on Calvary in a broken body upon a cross. It is the same love
which today pardons our sin, casts out our fear, sustains us in

faith and hope and is our Lord's supreme command to those who follow him.

Healing as Integration

'These days, Jan treats her body like a temple of the soul. She buys it Siberian ginseng, Selenium and vitamin E compounds and extract of the green-lipped Pacific mussel. She enhances it with cosmetics tested without cruelty to cat, frog or rabbit. She worries about it.'[1] Those words from a recent newspaper article indicate the almost obsessive and, some would say, unhealthy interest in 'health' in western society today. What is being referred to in this context is physical well-being, a concern for the body. This may or may not be healthy in itself. For fundamental to the nature of health is the fact that those who possess it are scarcely conscious of it and certainly not preoccupied with it. The healthier we are the less concerned we are with what is good, less good or bad in terms of health promotion. That may be part of the reason why it is often so difficult to convince young people of the damaging effects of drink or drug abuse and smoking. It is not until the health is already seriously impaired that people begin to look more carefully into these things.

The problem is not made any easier by the fact that we do not always agree on what we mean by 'health'. Certainly it must be more than just satisfactory physical functioning. There have been many attempts to define health but, alas, most of them tend to do so in individualistic, rather than corporate terms. The word 'health' was first brought to Britain by Anglo-saxon invaders and was used in the translation of the Psalms and Gospels. The root comes from the Western Teutonic *hal* which means whole and gives us the adjectives 'whole', 'hale' and 'holy', as well as 'healthy'. By derivation, then, the word 'healthy' means wholeness or soundness. The World Health

Organisation in 1948 defined health as 'a state of complete physical, mental and social well-being and not merely the absence of disease or infirmity'. So here it is seen as being something more than just physical. It includes the categories of mental and social. It points to an ideal: health is a goal to be achieved. It fails, however, to define what is meant by 'complete well-being'.

In classical Greek thought the idea of well-being was that of equilibrium or harmony achieved when the four humours of the body were all present in correct proportion: blood, phlegm, black bile and yellow bile. Probably the best-known definition of health in Roman literature is that given by Juvenal in his tenth Satire where he advises prayer for 'Mens sana in corpore sano' – a sound mind in a sound body.[2] Here again, however, the definition makes no allowance for the corporate aspects of health and welfare. One may legitimately ask just how far, in our present understanding of the meaning of health, these definitions are really sufficient. The question of whether we are able to function adequately as healthy human beings depends upon more than the answers we bring individually to the question. In a report 'The Health Divide – Inequalities in Health in the 1980s',[3] Margaret Whitehead has shown how questions like housing conditions, schools, family income, conditions of labour, unemployment, social and racial relationships can themselves be productive of ill health, whatever the individual stance may be. So a regime of *mens sana in corpore sano* can be both a short-sighted and indeed tough one for the individual unless it is balanced by the wider perspective of 'in societate sana'. That is to say, it is much more difficult for us to live a healthy life if we are living in a deprived and unhealthy society. The issue is even further complicated for the Christian, as we shall see later, by the need to distinguish between a secular and a Christian concept of health.

THE PROBLEM OF ALIENATION

Certainly health in its fullest sense is about harmony, and involves relationships between different systems of our being and between ourselves and other persons and elements in our environment. In this sense it is true that none of us know perfect health. We are in fact usually more conscious of our fragility than our health, of our alienation than our wholeness. F. W. Dillistone, echoing Hegel's concept of alienation, writes: 'Man is in conflict with nature, estranged from his fellow, he is alien from his own essence and end.'[4] Other writers and artists in the twentieth century seem to echo this concern about human loneliness and alienation, as they see the collapse of community, the breakdown of tradition, the declining confidence in education, law, life-long relationships and an informed religion, with the impact of modern technology and the materialism of modern life. With this goes an intense longing for some form of personal integration by which the separate and disparate elements in human life and in society can be brought together into some kind of harmonious whole.

Dillistone goes on to identify the chief components of the human structural situation at all times and all places. First of all, as human beings we are related to the all-encompassing environment: nature, life, God. The nuclear disaster at Chernobyl, the recent pronouncements of the ecology lobby and the fact that each political party is anxious to be seen to espouse the cause of the 'Greens' – all these indicate on a purely secular level the importance of this particular relationship. Those who see things from a religious perspective might recognise in the biblical story of Adam and Eve's Fall, with subsequent banishment from Eden, a form of alienation at this primary structural level.

Secondly, we are related in a more specialised way to the particular society to which we belong. We all know how a difficult relationship with someone at work, in the local club or church, can seriously undermine our tranquillity and possibly even our health. Morton Kelsey refers to the case of John Hunter, a famous surgeon, who, when sick with angina pectoris and aware of the influence of psychic disturbance on his physical condition, said that his life was in the hands of any rascal in London who chose 'to put him in a passion'.[5] He went on to prove his point by dying after a hospital board meeting!

Thirdly, there are relationships within the intimate family

group. We all know the uncomfortable feeling we experience when there is discord within the family. Sometimes we can even locate the area of discomfort within the chest, as though we had taken one too many dumplings at dinner and one of these had never properly gone down! We have probably also seen people go shuttling in and out of psychiatric hospitals and, in spite of the very best treatment available, remain defiantly unwell because there is a deep problem of unhappy or broken relationships at the root of their trouble. I remember receiving a letter from a young wife on the breakdown of her marriage, in which she said sadly: 'Breakdown in human relationships seems to be a disease of the space-age!'

Finally, there is that relationship to the inner world of personality, a world which may include conscious and unconscious elements. A great deal of human sickness may be due to a fracture at this level. True health means harmony at each of these levels and between them. Wherever there is a breakdown at any one of them, then there is need for some kind of rescue, redemption, healing. The Bible suggests that alienation has to give way to at-one-ment, that God has already taken the initiative in sending his Son, Jesus Christ, to bring us to reconciliation and renewal in him. Paul, in his letter to the Colossians, sees this divine act of reconciliation as extending to the whole created universe. All relationships are to be restored as we respond to the divine initiative in Jesus Christ. The promise is that by associating ourselves with the life, death and resurrection of Jesus we can begin to know that metanoia, that new orientation, which is the harbinger of 'life in all its fullness'. For now no situation is impervious to his love, no sickness is unto death in the old sense. We have with us Christ who is the great physician, and when we are truly united with him, then we know his healing power.

WHAT ARE WE?

Fully to grasp the meaning and truth of this kind of renewal, we need perhaps to take a rather more developed view of what we are and how we function. In the eighteenth and nineteenth centuries both the physical world and the human being were thought of in mechanistic terms. Everything about us could be explained in terms of mechanism, albeit a very complicated mechanism. In the nineteenth century Pasteur introduced the idea that the human being was not so much a mechanism as a battleground. A sick person represented an organism which was being sabotaged by pathogenic micro-organisms, germs. In the early part of this century there was a growing tendency to think of the body as an engine which had to be fuelled with the right kinds of food, water and vitamins. It is perfectly true that each of these models does tell us something important about ourselves. There is a sense in which my body has something of the character of a machine. If I fall over and break my leg, I need the bone reset in a splint or plaster cast. Much as I deplore the use of this model in human terms, it does seem to be a mechanical solution to a mechanical problem. Or again, if I have a cold, I am very much aware that a battle is going on within my physical being and will take such measures and dosages as will enable the right side to win. In the same way, I know that unless I maintain a reasonable intake of food and water, then I cannot expect my body to function properly. Over the past fifty years or so, however, there has been a growing recognition that, though such models provide some illumination into what we are, they do not tell the whole story. They are much too simple to give an accurate picture of what we are, or are meant to be.

By the 1950s medical science had shown that the chief culprit in certain diseases was not the foreign invader but the organism's inability to cope with it, a failure in the immune system, or an impairment often caused by stress or sheer human misery. We now know that the mind, and especially the emotional life, may have a part to play in triggering off major illness or in the ability to resist certain diseases. It is now generally recognised that good human relationships are important for health; that anxiety, guilt and despair can be disruptive of health; and that faith, hope and love are life-enhancing. The thrust of medical research confirms the importance of interpersonal factors in health and sickness and shows how one person may present in his/her illness the sickness of a whole group of people – perhaps the family, perhaps the whole neighbourhood or nation. Bob Lambourne, working from the Hebrew idea of corporate personality and Paul's affirmation 'as in Adam all die, so also in Christ shall all be made alive,'[6] speaks of the recognition within medicine today of the corporate nature of illness:

> The husband's peptic ulcer is as much a symptom of the wife's tension headache as her tension headache is a symptom of his ulcer; her anxiety and fears of pregnancy may be contributing as much to his peptic ulcer as his guilt over illicit activities and consequent aggression does to her headaches; what is sick is their relationship to each other and to others.[7]

HOW DO WE FUNCTION?

When we look at human functioning in more general terms we see that there is a remarkable sense of order about the processes of the body which govern the well-being of the individual. Whilst medical science can describe the processes at work, it is still largely ignorant about the fundamental factors which initiate the chemical responses which govern and control the body's functioning. Behind and beyond the phenomenon of healing, it does seem that there is some subtle power (the *vis medicatrix naturae*) which is inexplicable in terms of present biological and physical knowledge. It appears to be related to the emotional and mental life of the person, and this in turn is dependent upon a whole host of interlocking attitudes, purposes and relationships.

Traditionally it has been assumed that there are four levels of function on which the human being operates. There is the physical body; emotions that stimulate action; mind that investigates and controls events and monitors the environment; and some deeper level of moral influence often called the soul. This has sometimes been seen as the centre of integration which informs the mind, cleanses and purifies emotion and renews the body with strength and vitality. However, it is now recognised that any such division within the soul-body relationship is likely to lead to a dangerous misunderstanding of what we are and how we function. William Watty poses the question:

> What happens to the human being when his body is seen as a combination of parts, with the emphasis on the parts? What happens to man when his biology does not communicate with his psychology, or his psychology with his sociology? What happens when his anthropological determinants are in conflict with his theology? Can we really understand the meaning of health without seeing man in his integrity and in the wholeness of his being and the nexus of his total relationship?[8]

We have referred to the remarkable sense of order that normally governs the well-being of the individual. The converse of all this is the disorganisation which precedes disintegration. This, it seems, usually follows stressful situations, emotional upheavals, disappointment, betrayal, bereavement, loss of meaning and loss of worth. Research in the field of psychosomatic medicine has shown that envy, hatred and suppressed anger can change the structure of the stomach's lining, alter the clotting time of the blood, and that emotional changes in the person bring observable physical change in every part of the body. It is also perhaps worth reminding ourselves that somato-psychic effects are just as powerful and important as psycho-somatic effects. In other words, the body influences the mind just as the mind influences the body.

TOTAL HEALTH CARE

As there are certain matters to which we must pay attention if we are to remain physically in good shape – by this I mean things like proper exercise and rest, fresh air and good food – so there is a particular ordering of the psychic or spiritual life to which we attend if we are to know health in its widest sense. We must therefore be concerned that our thoughts, our feelings, our memories, our emotions are properly ordered, expressed and kept in tune with God's will and purpose. Writing to his friends in the church in Philippi, the apostle Paul suggests a programme of health care which begins with the counsel to rejoice in the Lord, to show magnanimity to all, knowing that the Lord is at hand. His solution for anxiety is prayer and there follows in brief compass a whole philosophy of prayer:

> Have no anxiety about anything, but in everything by prayer and supplication with thanksgiving let your requests be made known to God. And the peace of God, which passes all understanding, will keep your hearts and your minds in Christ Jesus.

As the human mind will always set itself on something, then let it be set on the right things:

> Whatever is true, whatever is honorable, whatever is just, whatever is pure, whatever is lovely, whatever is gracious, if there is any excellence, if there is anything worthy of praise, think about these things. What you have learned and received and heard and seen in me, do; and the God of peace [shalom] will be with you.[9]

The association between mental and emotional life and physical condition is not new but has been noted since the time of Galen, the outstanding physician of the Roman era, who reported that cancer was more frequent in 'melancholic' than in 'sanguine' women.[10] From studies done by Dr L. LeShan and Dr Caroline Thomas in the USA and by Dr S. Greer in the UK, it has been suggested that there may be some correlation between certain personality types and the development of cancer. Many cancer sufferers, it seems, are people whose early childhood experiences have led them to undervalue themselves and repress both their needs and their feelings. Of course, not everyone of this type develops cancer, any more than do all heavy smokers. It seems, however, that when such a person experiences a loss, like bereavement, the body's immune system becomes depressed and so is unable to cope with cancer cells which would normally be destroyed by a happy, healthy system. Other researchers have noticed a correlation between cancer and feelings of hopelessness, frustration and family difficulties. Sir William Osler, a great medical teacher of his day, at a time when tuberculosis was the great scourge of the world's city-dwellers, warned his profession that the fate of the tubercular depended more on what they had in their heads than on what was in their chests.[11]

A GROWING UNDERSTANDING

If there is at present much that is not completely understood, there is today a more general reaching out to, and acceptance of, the concept of the wholeness of the human being and the wholeness of life. Research into the immune system, endocrinology and its mechanisms, endorphins (the body's own internal pain-control mechanism), seems to underline the need carefully to consider the close relationship of body, mind and spirit and to see them as aspects of the whole being. With this goes also the need to treat the individual in relation to the community and to offer such support and spiritual help to enable that individual to respond positively to life with all its ambiguity, complexity, suffering and sin.

This has long been the understanding of those in Africa and many other non-Western societies. Dr Margaret Read, in discussing the Navaho Indians of North America, writes:

> While the doctors could rid the body of pain and drive out the germs which were the cause of infection, for the religious Navaho this was not enough. The religious and psychological support of the Navaho curer was frequently needed by the patient in order to gain correct balance in the total environment.[12]

For the Navaho Indian, health is the result of a correct relationship between the individual and the total environment and that includes the supernatural environment. Illness bears evidence of a disturbance, a falling out of harmony with life. Those with experience of dealing with sick people recognise that one of the prime needs of those who are ill is for the assurance of reconciliation: reconciliation to God, to self, to family and friends and to the world around them. This reconciliation must penetrate all levels of experience. We know that we cannot be completely reconciled to God without an awareness that God's way must be our way and his concerns our concerns. For Jesus this meant incarnation, ministry, agony, crucifixion, dereliction and resurrection. All these stages are important and at some point they touch our own lives in some degree. The important question for us is whether throughout these varied experiences, we possess a centre which is focused upon God. This means that we have to give time and space for that which integrates, brings wholeness, unity of being and purpose.

Jesus responded to a complaint that it was by the prince of demons that he cast out demons by saying: 'Every kingdom divided against itself is laid waste, and no city or house divided against itself will stand . . .'[13] I see this as a dominical assurance that both inner life and outer life, the body and soul, must be one in union with God. St Mark brings confirmation of this truth in his story of the man who was healed with a little help from his friends.[14] When Jesus saw the paralysed man he said, 'My son, your sins are forgiven.' When the scribes questioned Jesus' right to forgive sins, he responded, 'Which is easier, to say to the paralytic, "Your sins are forgiven", or to say, "Rise, take up your pallet and walk"?' To the paralysed man he said, 'I say to you, rise, take up your pallet and go home.' To everyone's amazement he did exactly that. So Jesus performed the miracle they could see in order to demonstrate that he had performed another miracle that they could not see – the fact that his sins were forgiven. This, it seems, was the man's chief need and the healing was a guarantee in their own terms that Jesus could offer just that. If sometimes it seems easier to pray for something which we describe as being 'spiritual' rather than for something which we describe as being 'physical', we should remember that in God's sight there is no such distinction. In his sight we are one, body, mind and spirit, and we are meant to be whole, not fragmented and divided.

The great challenge of spirituality in our day is how we can become whole persons, uniting our physicality and our spirituality, our bodies and our souls, in harmonious unity within ourselves, within the network of relationships God has determined for us, and with God himself, through his Son, Jesus Christ. Something of our difficulty in this is faced by Grace Jantzen, in her study of Julian of Norwich. She refers to Julian's parable of the lord and the servant and the ways in which sin – the fracturing of the personality – leads to sins. Among the most striking of these to Julian's mind is the blindness which the servant suffered when he fell into the ditch. His whole perspective was distorted in a threefold way. In the first place, he was blinded to his lord's loving compassion, because he concentrated entirely upon his own distress. Secondly, he was blinded to his continued worth in his lord's sight. Third, because he was blinded to himself and his own worth in the sight of his lord, he was also blinded to his own deepest nature and was unable to recognise that in spite of what had happened he still longed to serve his lord.[15] Here we see how crucial is the acceptance of that forgiveness which is by grace alone, if we are to know true healing, and the recovery of that relationship with God which transcends, informs and enriches all the rest.

It is important also to remember that we all suffer from a fatal disease – a common one we call mortality. From time to time we are made painfully aware of this: that our hold on life is frail and that at some time we shall have to let go even of this. Under such circumstances the wise are those who constantly rejoice in those things that make life worth living and those relationships that make it worthwhile. The secret, very difficult for us to learn, then lies in discovering how growth comes by letting go. For the time will come when the Lord will call upon us to let go of life itself. If the growing and letting go have been successfully completed, that will be a time of true integration, healing and shalom.

4

Healing Miracles

Perhaps the chief difficulty about miracles is not whether they do or do not happen, but that they do not always happen when we want them or in the way that we would choose. Of course there are those who deny absolutely any possibility of miracle. The world, they say, is constituted in such a way that suspensions, interventions, incursions cannot possibly take place. Much depends on whether we see the universe as a closed 'Newtonian' system, where nothing can happen which does not fit in with the so-called laws of the universe, or an open system which responds to the movement of the transcendent within the regularity of known laws. It seems likely that the old mechanistic interpretation of life with fixed and immutable laws is steadily giving way to a more fluid conception of life and matter. The principle of coherence, however, is important and one that should be given serious consideration. Few of us would want to live in a world where Nature was entirely capricious and without any known pattern or order.

It has also to be allowed that often what makes an event miraculous is the way in which it is interpreted. An Anglican priest recently appeared on television against the background of a vicarage which had been almost completely destroyed during a very severe storm. He and his wife had emerged shaken but unhurt. 'You were lucky,' said the reporter. 'No,' said the vicar, 'I'm a minister of religion. It was a miracle!' People do rejoice in the emotion of wonder and surprise. There seems to be a need to be able to describe the rare events which cause us wonder and thanksgiving in terms of miracle. A miracle, then, is a rare event or combination of events which has distinctive elements of deliverance and wonder, as, for example, the Israelites' crossing of the Red Sea.

TRUE OR FALSE?

This does not mean that we accept every account of miracle as being true. There is always the need to balance what we know of the laws of nature with the testimony of those who have experienced miracle. We have also to remember the cautionary word of that redoubtable philosopher, David Hume, who suggested that miracles tend chiefly to be found among 'uncivilised' and primitive peoples. He also warned that different religions appeal to the miraculous to establish faith and in the process ultimately discredit faith.

We may not find it possible to accept as literal truth every account of the miracles recorded in the New Testament, not if we have a proper understanding of the role and meaning of myth and legend. This does not mean that we deny the religious truth behind them. Many of those stories have an important religious meaning, if only we can discover it, even if we have doubts about the historical accuracy of some. I confess to finding the story of the coin in the fish's mouth rather difficult to take.[1] Peter reminds Jesus that they have to pay the yearly half-shekel tax due for the maintenance of the temple. Jesus tells him to catch a fish. In its mouth will be a shekel coin which will pay the tax for both of them. My difficulty about this is that it portrays Jesus as a kind of street-wise wonder-worker. This just does not fit the rest of the picture which the Gospel writers present to us. Certainly it does not ring true with Jesus' response to the temptation in the wilderness, when he deliberately refused to turn stones into bread in order to encourage a popularist response.[2] Of course this reference to a fish and a coin might well have been just a kind of jokey aside that later was built into the tradition as an actual happening. Equally, wise and careful biblical interpretation might lead us to conclude that the feeding of the five thousand is to be seen more as a sacrament of sharing than a miracle of multiplication. The really fascinating and challenging thing about the miracles of Jesus, and not least the healing miracles, is that people felt that they were in the presence not of a great magician, but of one in whom the love and the power of God were seen and known. I see no reason to doubt that Jesus restored sight to the blind, helped deaf people to hear, enabled the lame to walk, cleansed people of disabling diseases and delivered those who were thought to be possessed by evil spirits. I see these largely as signs of the dawning of a new age within the kingly rule of God.

The Christian cannot escape the challenge of the miraculous. As I once heard the late T. W. Manson say to a group of students: 'If you can accept the miracle of the Incarnation and the Resurrection, why quibble about a few loaves and fishes!' If we accept the fact of a Creator God who has established the world according to certain prescribed laws of nature, then he who wills those laws may equally will their suspension or, more probably, their extension in ways beyond our understanding. If we go on to consider that this same God made himself known in Jesus Christ who came to initiate the kingly rule of God over all creation, then we should be prepared for some signs and wonders.

A RARE OCCURRENCE

The real problem about miracles, however, is not that they happen but that they happen so infrequently. I suppose that in the nearly forty years I have been involved in this ministry I have seen only five or six healings which I would describe as 'miraculous', but scores where one could identify many of the processes involved.

I recall a service for healing in a church very near to my own, where, after the laying on of hands, one woman just sobbed uncontrollably. At the close of the service, I invited her into the vestry. We talked together; I listened to her story; we prayed together and then, after half an hour or so, we left the church. I confess that I forgot all about her until the following Thursday when she telephoned to say how sorry she was for any embarrassment she might have caused me. She said that she had felt dreadfully ill. On the Monday her condition deteriorated and she became very anxious about herself. However by Tuesday she began to feel better. On Wednesday she went to the doctor and told him to take her off the drugs he was giving her for three different conditions. The doctor expressed surprise and asked her what had happened. When she told him that she had been to a service for healing at her church, he became uneasy. 'Are you sure that you should come off medication?' he asked. 'Oh yes,' said the woman. 'I feel better than I have for years!' At this point in the conversation, I interrupted and suggested that perhaps it was a little premature to give up all medical treatment. 'Oh no', she replied. 'I'm like that little boy in the Bible who had to get worse before he got better. I am better now.'

I saw this woman twelve months later, when I was conducting a church parade service at the same church. She came to me after the service, looking very smart in her Guide uniform and said happily, 'It's just twelve months ago, Mr Dale, and I am feeling better than I have for years.'

I think I understand something of what happened in that service. Somehow God spoke to that woman, releasing her from burdens and anxieties which had troubled her deeply and resulted in physical symptoms of a very distressing and disabling kind. I recognise that deliverance as a work of God but would not necessarily describe it as a miracle, though I would not quarrel with those who do. A miracle of healing is for me a breaking through of God's recreating and renewing power in ways which effect remarkable cure and which provoke wonder and surprise. Here I saw not so much a supernatural intervention of a miraculous kind, but rather the working out of processes which I can to some degree understand in psycho/physical terms. I can still thank God for this deliverance, as I can for the growing understanding of its nature.

I have also seen situations where there has been unceasing prayer and splendid care for the patient and the disease has just pursued its inexorable course. If God does intervene, it is on a very rare occasion and it appears to bear no relation to the faith or worthiness of the patient or the petitioner. Just think of the prayers that were offered for the evangelist, David

Watson, when he was suffering from terminal cancer. Think also of what it would have done for true religion if he had been spared whilst countless others were not cured.

But is the word 'intervention' an appropriate one to use in such a situation? Surely what we look for in the God and Father of our Lord Jesus Christ is not one who exercises power arbitrarily and unpredictably, without any norm by which we can assess his action. What we look for is one who is faithful to the promises he has made and to the love which he has shown in Jesus Christ; in other words, a God whose character guarantees the integrity, consistency and coherence of all that he does.

Augustine wrestled with this problem and, in *De Civitate Dei* (*Concerning the City of God*), expressed the view: 'Miracle therefore does not happen against nature but against nature as we know it . . . for can what happens in the will of God be opposed to nature since in any case the will of such a great Creator is the nature of everything created?'[3]

NATURAL AND SUPERNATURAL

If Augustine is saying that 'nature as we know it' is not nature as it is, then we are left with another problem. But if the will of the Creator is consistent with his nature as all-powerful, benevolent and loving, whose nature determines his action, then natural law and divine intervention are bound together in the one being. We then have some guarantee that that which goes beyond the experience of the everyday has some coherence with the whole. God's faithfulness to his own nature makes any absolute distinction between natural and supernatural unnecessary. All is of God and God is good.

We know that the healing process appears to be generally natural and law-abiding. There would be no medical science if this were not so. What are described as miracles are the outward and visible signs of the ways of God which are beyond our understanding. They tell us something more of the nature, movement and direction of the spiritual reality which moves constantly in and through the physical reality. If we cannot always follow the process of causation, we can try to discover its meaning.

It is one of the misconceptions about the Church's ministry of healing that a medically unexplained healing is more wonderful than one brought about by medical means. It is true that familiarity breeds complacency, if not contempt. We take for granted the day-to-day work of our GPs, our hospitals and National Health Service. Whilst doctors generally would deny that they actually heal, they do open the way for healing to take place and are often responsible for many miracles of the commonplace.

Healing in the Old Testament, like salvation, is seen in the context of God's acts of blessing. These are grounded in creation, and are seen not in isolated and unusual events but as continuously operating through human life from conception, through birth, growth and maturity. Healing is also part of God's act of blessing and it is normally a process rather than a single event. Professor D. C. Westerman has pointed out that healing from an illness was experienced quite naturally as God's deed. Equally:

> The difference between natural healing and healing through the miraculous intervention of a man of God is only relative, because in both cases God is the one who heals . . . It is a misunderstanding to think that healing from illness can have theological significance only when it is miraculous, or that only miracle healings bring one into contact with God. In the Bible, God's healing power is active in every recovery.[4]

All this points to the way in which medicine today has become secularised and lost any connection with theology. It also indicates the degree to which we have departed from the insights of the Bible with its basic assumption that the relationship with God simply belongs to the nature of our existence. That there were in biblical times special salvation events in which the relationship was particularised and heightened must not be denied. The deliverance out of Egypt was one such special event in which God's mercy for the oppressed who cry out to him was graciously made manifest. For the Christian, the incarnation, ministry, death and resurrection of Jesus Christ are seen as a single, though complex, act of particularity.

In general, however, we lose something of great importance when we fail to see salvation and healing as a process, and a natural process rather than a once-for-all particular act. It is a process which restores the individual, or the community, to the wholeness of life which is God's will for them. The greatest threat to their existence is separation from God through their falling away from him.

NAAMAN'S HEALING

The biblical account of the healing of Naaman may serve as a useful illustration of the way in which God can speak and act in and through the natural, as well as in the supernatural.[5] Naaman was a commander in the army of the King of Syria, a kind of Montgomery of the ancient world. Yet he had contracted leprosy, an embarrassing condition for one of Naaman's social standing. Naaman's wife had an Israelite servant girl who knew of Elisha, the prophet of Israel, and suggested that if Naaman were to go to Elisha he would almost certainly be healed of his leprosy. Eventually, after some misunderstanding and a bit of high-level diplomacy, Naaman arrived with full panoply of horses and chariots. Without even seeing him, Elisha sent a messenger saying, 'Go and wash in the Jordan seven times, and your flesh shall be restored, and you shall be clean.' Naaman felt that this cavalier kind of treatment was unfitting to his dignity and an insult to his king. This healer might at least have gone through the motions which these magicians usually employed; but simply to be told to go and bathe in some river, as though he were a beggar with no idea of personal hygiene, was scarcely appropriate! In any case, why should a Syrian nobleman go and bathe in that Jewish river? If he must bathe in a river to be healed, surely there were other rivers just as therapeutic in his own land of Syria.

Naaman went away in a rage, muttering, 'I thought that he would surely come out to me, and stand, and call on the name of the Lord his God, and wave his hand over the place, and cure the leper.' Fortunately Naaman's servants were wiser than their master in this instance and said:

> My father, if the prophet had commanded you to do some great thing, would you not have done it? How much rather, then, when he says to you, "Wash and be clean"?

Naaman was persuaded, went down and dipped himself seven times in the Jordan, as Elisha had prescribed and his flesh was restored 'like the flesh of a little child, and he was clean'. Naaman then returned to Elisha, stood before him and said:

> Behold, I know that there is no God in all the earth but in Israel; so accept now a present from your servant.

Elisha would have none of this; it was God who had healed. So Naaman asked:

> I pray you, let there be given to your servant two mules' burden of earth; for henceforth your servant will not offer burnt offering or sacrifice to any god but the Lord.

There are two things to be noticed about this story. First, there is the emphasis that is put upon the natural way in which the healing had occurred. Naaman had expected an impressive piece of magic or to be asked to do some particularly demanding thing. All that was required was a piece of everyday behaviour – to wash in the Jordan seven times. Secondly, there is the recognition that it is God who heals and Naaman has come to the true God. He now knows that he has to stay in relation with this God, hence his request for two mules' burden of earth from the land of Israel: 'for henceforth your servant will not offer burnt offering or sacrifice to any god but the Lord.' Here we see that healing means new life, a fresh stance, a life that has to be lived before God.

GUIDING PRINCIPLES

So we arrive at certain principles behind miracles. First, they do not occur in the abstract but always in a religious context and within an atmosphere of faith. This does not mean that the faith is always that of the one who benefits from the miracle. Second, they do not consist of random effects but have the characteristic of conveying something about God. This essentially is how I see the miracles of Jesus. They speak to us of God's love for all creation; just as all creation bears the weight of his glory, so it must ultimately bear the marks of his love. They speak of the nature of that human brokenness in relation to which God's saving action in Jesus Christ becomes effective. They also indicate God's purpose to restore and make whole that which is distorted and divided. Third, to accept miracle we have to presuppose God; for miracles only make sense in an existing area of faith. The history of the Christian Church would seem to confirm that miracles take place more readily in those days and in those places where faith is vital and God a living reality.

OUR ATTITUDE TO MIRACLES TODAY

Professor Hayek, the economist, in a Channel Four broadcast in 1984, suggested that there is a need today to give a rational justification for an anti-rationalist attitude. The anti-rationalism he was supporting is the case for beliefs and attitudes that stem from religion, rather than from science. He was suggesting that there are truths that speak to us in our humanity which belong to a deeper level of experience than our speculation and popular scientism. The interplay of body, mind and spirit is still a relatively unexplored field, so there are bound to be phenomena not yet explicable in terms of current knowledge. Constantly we are discovering new understanding of the way in which God interacts with his creation. This can be related to, without being determined by, the latest developments in scientific and philosophical thought. The God who is both immanent in his creation and yet transcends it will always have new ways of surprising and blessing his people. So, for the Christian, reason apart from revelation is inadequate. Phenomena that do not fit comfortably with the human power of rationalisation may always present themselves, since there are forms of knowledge which are unattainable to the finite mind. Peter Ackroyd, the novelist, reflecting upon the mystery of time and human origins, wrote: 'All our learning really amounts to no more than stories told in the dark. Wonderful stories, sometimes . . . but stories, nevertheless.'[6] Heaven help us if we ever reach the point where there is no occasion for wonder and worship, or we fail to rejoice in the fact that all life is a miracle. Finally, it is perhaps worth recalling that it was not on the grounds of miracles alone that the Early Church rested its faith in Christ but on the supreme miracle of the resurrection. Miracles were the active signs of the power of God to bring life from death and victory from defeat, and a sequel to that surpassing wonder.

Many Faces, Many Forms

It is perhaps not too much to state that there is at the present time a spiritual and ecological crisis on our planet. We may have come through the cold war between East and West to discover that there is an even more serious threat facing us in terms of pollution and a chronic misuse of the world's resources. This, together with the rapid and disturbing rate of change in social, political and religious affairs, has produced a disturbance of faith and the onset of a kind of existential fear (anxiety which arises from our life in the world).

This anxiety permeates our being and hangs like a dark shadow over our world, producing a reaction in terms of fear on the one hand and a longing for certitude and security on the other. In our society today there are those who rejoice in the liberation which new knowledge brings and in the mastery of the environment which comes with advancing technology. There are others, however, who, perhaps because they have been damaged more than most by their experience of life, flee from the freedom which new knowledge brings and the possibility of a creative personal response to the problems which beset us by turning to simplistic, directed, religious (or political) solutions offered by authoritarian figures and pseudo-messiahs. There may be a sense in which most of us swing rather uncertainly between these two attitudes. Then we need to recall that faith, being one of the prime religious virtues, can never travel alone but is always at its best when accompanied by truth and love. It is also salutary to recall that not all forms of religious belief are unqualified expressions of the good. This present spiritual crisis, like the sickness crisis of which it is a part, presents us with an exciting opportunity to grow in faith, hope and love, and in Paul's celebrated and succinct statement of the work of salvation, to 'work out your own salvation with fear and trembling; for God is at work in you, both to will and to work for his good pleasure.'[1]

It is against that kind of background that I want to consider briefly some of the non-medical ways of attempting to meet human sickness and need. Many of these, it seems to me, have arisen as a reaction to a failure of the Church to fulfil its historic ministry of healing. One of the most pressing questions facing us in the Christian healing ministry is how we are to estimate these various movements and methods of healing. In so doing we have to ask ourselves what is the picture of God which is presented by each of these various forms of healing.

CHRISTIAN SCIENCE

Christian Science is a religious movement concerned chiefly with the deliverance of healing by prayer alone. It denies sin and the sacrifice of Christ as atonement for sin; and at the same time denies the reality of disease and pain. The only reality is Mind or Spirit. Christian Science was founded by Mary Baker Eddy. She herself had been a chronic invalid who had been influenced and healed by a mesmerist, Phineas Quimby of Maine. Even before she met Quimby, however, she had written 'all disease is in the mind', adding 'as disease is what follows the error, destroy the cause and the effect will cease'. After Quimby's death, Mrs Eddy went on to develop her own theory, presenting it in her book *Science and Health* (1875). Coming at a time when both the Church and orthodox medicine ignored many biblical insights about the mind/body relationship, the book had an enthusiastic reception and went through many editions. In 1879 the first 'Church of Christ Scientist' was opened in Boston, Massachusetts.

Mary Baker Eddy's teaching can be summarised in the following way:

> God is all in all.
> God is good. God is mind.
> God, spirit, being all, nothing is matter.

These propositions, she observes, are equally understood when read backwards, which proves their correspondence with truth![2] This philosophy of Idealism is quite ancient. It re-embodies the ancient heresy of Docetism which, as it denied the reality of matter, also denied that Jesus was manifested in the flesh or that he actually suffered on the cross. Christian orthodoxy has always found Christian Science, as Mrs Eddy propounded it, difficult to accept. If health, life and pleasure are a part of reality, we cannot say that illness, pain, suffering and death are not real but just projections of the mind. Equally it is difficult for us to accept that we must avoid doctors, surgery and vaccines whilst we accept mental suggestion. Indeed, many ministers and doctors will know of the amount of mischief that has been done to dangerously ill people who have been persuaded by followers of this sect not to seek medical assistance until it was almost too late. It must be said that not all Christian Scientists have totally eschewed conventional medicine. That there are many cures which have been effected by Christian Scientists working on the purely mental plane cannot be denied. Few Christians would want to quarrel with Mary Baker Eddy's credo in *Science and Health* and inscribed on the wall of many a Christian Science church: 'Divine love has always met and always will meet every human need.' The movement certainly filled a need which orthodox Christianity and traditional medicine of its time were refusing to recognise. If the churches had been more sympathetic to the possibilities of the healing movement started by Mrs Eddy, they might have been able to contain and correct whatever errors, theological or otherwise, were inherent in it. When the churches refused to listen to her message, Mrs Eddy was led to found her own. It is a not unfamiliar story and a sad one of theological or ecclesiastical rigidity being responsible for the development of yet another sect.

Today one of the best informed and conducted daily newspapers in the USA is *The Christian Science Monitor*, which has recently produced a very balanced Special Report on 'Christian Healing Today'. Even so, it would be difficult for Christians to accept as part of the Church's ministry of healing a movement whose teaching on the unreality of matter, sin and suffering conflicts with the biblical doctrines of the creation, fall and redemption.

SPIRITUALISM

This is a name which covers a number of different organisations, systems of belief and practice. All forms of Spiritualism unite in asserting the survival of the dead and believe that it is both possible and acceptable to establish communication with the spirits of the dead. In its modern form, Spiritualism dates from the occult experiences of the Fox family in America in 1848. It soon spread to Britain and Europe as a reaction against the prevalent materialism. It has found followers amongst recognised scholars such as Oliver Lodge, F. W. H. Myers and W. F. Prince. The practice of Spiritualism is denounced by Scripture (Deut. 18:11) and by all branches of the Christian Church. In this country the Spiritualist Churches claim to be fully Christian in outlook and hold Sunday services with prayers of intercession for those who are sick and also special services for healing. Many who have failed to find the comfort of such services in the more orthodox churches have been drawn into Spiritualist worship only to find themselves disturbed by the element of clairvoyance which is also part of that tradition.

It is usually held that faith is unnecessary in either the healer or the patient. The healing offered is by laying on of hands or, at a distance, by prayer and thought transference or with the use of a radionic instrument. In this country one of the best-known healers in the Spiritualist tradition was Harry Edwards, who developed his own healing centre at Shere in Surrey and did effect remarkable cures, especially in people with arthritis, joint injuries and physical malformations. It has to be said that he, and the National Federation of Spiritual Healers to which he belonged, received little recognition by the medical profession in his time.

The Confederation of Healing Organisations now includes the National Federation of Spiritual Healers, the Guild of Spiritualist Healers, the British Alliance of Healing Associations, the Spiritualist Association of Great Britain, the Spiritualists' National Union, the World Federation of Healing – altogether 7,500 healers from eighteen independent associations (mainly spiritual healers) who practise privately or in voluntary clinics. There are another 13,000 healers outside the C.H.O. The General Medical Council now permits doctors to refer patients to spiritual healers, providing the patient is willing. A recent survey by the Avon Health Authority indicated that seventeen per cent of GPs in that area are prepared to refer patients to healers.[3] Interest of doctors in this field seems to be increasing but there is little sign of general acceptance of Spiritualist claims within the medical profession. *Good Housekeeping* magazine recently caused a flutter in certain medical and ecclesiastical dovecotes by reporting that four London hospitals were using healers to treat AIDS patients. The C.H.O. is now raising £200,000 to establish clinical trials which it hopes will demonstrate that 'healing works'.

FAITH HEALING

It is difficult always to separate out the many forms of healing which might be included under this heading. One has only to attend the annual exhibition in London sponsored by the various healing agencies to see how multi-faceted is the healing movement in Britain today. There one can see and sample almost every form of 'healing' under the sun – Christian Science, Spiritualism, Psychic Healing, Naturopathy, Osteopathy, Radiesthesia, Health Foods, Blue Stone Healing and many more. All these in some way involve the response of faith. The question is: what kind of faith, and faith in what or whom?

As this question implies, there is an inherent element of ambiguity in the very concept of faith healing. Faith is a term which can be used in two distinct ways in the Christian context. First of all, there is the word used in an objective way to stand for the body of Christian truth. Then there is the more subjective application of faith as a response of trust to the truth as revealed in Jesus Christ. It is this sense of faith as the response of trust that is involved in Christian healing, rather than the ability 'to believe six impossible things before breakfast', as the Queen says to Alice in *Through the Looking-Glass*. This kind of faith goes along with hope and love, as one of the great theological virtues. It often implies an element of commitment, as in Abraham's going out into the unknown. In Paul's case it meant acceptance of God's 'No' as far as personal cure of his 'thorn in the flesh' was concerned. 'My grace is sufficient for you, for my power is made perfect in weakness' was God's reply to Paul's prayer for healing.[4]

All this is light years away from some of the concepts and strategies of 'faith healing', which often have less to do with faith, in Paul Tillich's sense of 'a state of being grasped by ultimate concern or, more specifically, by the Spiritual Presence', than with a kind of manipulative auto-suggestive process sometimes accompanied by communal hysteria and a dependence upon magic. For this reason, I confess that I am unhappy when people speak of the Christian healing ministry in terms of 'faith healing'. We are not in the business of evoking trust in ourselves, our methods and practices; still less with exerting psychic force or emotional pressure upon people in the name of healing. This is all too often the kind of impression that many have derived of faith healers and faith healing. This is not to suggest that all faith healers are rogues and charlatans. They are often good people with a genuine care for others, though few would be able to give an adequate explanation of what they are doing or for the hope they have in healing. It must be allowed that many faith healers have succeeded in alleviating much pain and suffering. Bruce Macmanaway discovered his gift for healing when in the army during the last war. He found that he could help wounded men simply by putting his hands on them. Pain disappeared, sometimes bleeding stopped and often there was no septicaemia, although there were no sterile dressings. He works on the assumption that a form of energy flows through him into the patient from some kind of 'higher intelligence'.

Dangers inherent in the faith healing approach and exemplified in the less scrupulous practitioners include that of exploiting human desperation in sickness, ignoring or depreciating medical scientific method and, by attributing any failure of result to the patient's lack of faith, seriously compounding the initial problem. Though we recognise the ambiguity which underlies all our attempts to minister in this field, we have to emphasise that Christian healing derives not from faith in a particular individual or method but from the 'healer's' conscious and deliberate relationship with, and dependence upon, the God and Father of our Lord Jesus Christ. Perhaps Tillich's cautionary word might be appropriate here:

> Magic healing, of which faith healing is a conspicuous form, is one of many ways of healing. In the name of the Spiritual Presence it can be neither unambiguously accepted nor unambiguously rejected. But three things must be stated with respect to it: first, that it is not healing through faith but by magic concentration; second, that it is justified as an element in many human encounters, though it has destructive as well as creative possibilities; and third, that if it excludes other ways of healing in principle (as some faith-healing movements and individuals do) it is predominantly destructive.[5]

EXORCISM

C. S. Lewis once wrote:

> There are two equal and opposite errors into which our race can fall about the devils. One is to disbelieve in their existence. The other is to believe, and to feel an excessive and unhealthy interest in them. They themselves are equally pleased by both errors, and hail a materialist or a magician with the same delight.

No one who has given thought to the human condition can deny that evil is a mystery that haunts our existence and has done so from earliest times. This is the crucial factor that lies behind the biblical story of Adam and Eve. It is the influence behind that sentence in the Lord's Prayer, 'Lead us not into temptation, but deliver us from evil'. This can be translated 'from the evil one' or 'from evil'. A study of the various recent translations reveals that they move to and fro between two alternatives. So the evil from which we pray to be delivered may be abstract or personal. If evil is abstract, as much current thinking would encourage us to believe, any question of conflict between good and evil becomes more or less academic. Then the sudden upsurge, or periodic depredations, of evil leave us baffled and shaken, for we have virtually denied its reality. On the other hand, there is the danger of seeing demons everywhere and demonstrating an undue fascination for them.

It is important to recognise that if we too lightly eliminate the dimension of the demonic, we are in danger of dismissing an important element in the teaching of Jesus. It is unlikely that Jesus would have taught his disciples to pray for deliverance from a power which had no real existence. He seems, in fact, to have accepted a robust belief in the demonic and operated within that frame of reference in many of his works of healing. Most of us today have had sufficient experience of the dark force of evil and its insidious power to penetrate all human life to compel us to recognise its objective reality.

The thought forms in which evil is seen today, however, are different from those of Jesus' day. We no longer operate within the same frame of reference, at least where medicine is concerned. Or could it be, as Canon Melinsky maintains:

Having been shown out of the front door by the white-coated clinician, the demons are entering the back door in the guise of anxiety and the despair of meaninglessness, racial and colour conflict, over-population and the squandering of the earth's natural resources. Are these the demons which the church of the twenty-first century will be called to cast out?[6]

Melinsky goes on to suggest that it was because he recognised the demonology of his day to be a variable, and to some degree, deceptive frame of reference that St John fails to give any account of the casting out of demons, whereas it was such an obvious feature of the Synoptics. John, after all, was concerned that his Gospel should have as universal an application as possible.

Until recently in this country there was little evidence of the practice of exorcism, or deliverance ministry, as it is now usually called. Whatever happened, happened quietly and it was all done with great circumspection. Now it seems to be much more widely practised and greater importance is accorded it within the armoury of the Church's healing ministry. This may be due in part to the rise of sects and cults devoted to occultism, witchcraft and satanism. The 1970s explosion of interest in such matters seems to have continued, after an initial dying away. Now the problem, it seems, is acute in many parts of the country. One might ask searching questions about the social, political and religious circumstances which encourage the growth of such interests, but this would not eliminate the problem.

I suppose my principal concern is about the language and thought-forms used and the frame of reference in which exorcism or deliverance is applied. It could be that the frame of reference, however deceptive, is a convenient one which enables the good to be identified and the evil to be dealt with. I confess to feeling very inadequate to deal with exorcism as a practice since it has played so very little part in my own ministry. Are we perhaps moving into a new time of spiritual darkness, when the Church has largely lost its grasp of people's hearts and lives, when pagan values have become more dominant, the occult has become more widely practised, and in which we need to look more carefully into questions of demonology and the practice of deliverance ministry?

It would plainly be wrong to say to someone who has been taken by the scruff of the neck and lifted out of a deadly subjugation to the demonic, that this is an illusion. It would also cast doubts upon the reality of the salvation experience. So it is important to look with sensitivity and sympathy to those who are practising deliverance ministry in an area of life and work in which many churches are completely impotent. We should, however, be aware of the possible pitfalls in this kind of ministry. There is, first of all, the danger of setting up a theological dualism in the mind of the sufferer. It is always possible to empower evil by the attention we pay to it and so to reaffirm the powers which Christ has dealt with so decisively on Calvary. Then there is the danger that by over-emphasis upon the demonic we may leave people with a world view in which superstition and magic remain supreme, with Christianity as just another, if more powerful, form of magic.

Evelyn Frost in her book *Christian Healing* points out that healings by exorcism in the first three centuries of the Church fall into two categories.[7] First, there are those healings where exorcism becomes necessary because there appear to be circumstances, people and places in which the activity of evil is more directly perceptible; where there is flagrant hostility to the good; and where the presence of evil can be markedly felt, with lives organised in opposition to God that radiate a known evil influence. Under such circumstances, where the forces of evil have full play, then the authority of Christ for the rebuke of sin was deemed necessary.

The second class of conditions in which exorcism was deemed necessary was in those diseases the symptoms of which can now be healed by known processes: for example, fever and certain types of epilepsy. The distinction seems to me to be an important one and might be further extended in the light of current medical and psychological knowledge. We now see that an otherwise healthy person, suffering from a feverish cold, does not require an exorcism so much as a hot bath, a warm drink and a couple of aspirins and perhaps a day in bed. Many of the ghosts which formerly troubled the human spirit have now been banished in favour of more scientifically intelligible processes.

That is not to say that we have banished the concept of evil, or that exorcism to counter the effects of that first category of evil is not necessary today. It may well be. My difficulty arises largely from Frost's second category of conditions. Some of the ideas by means of which the concepts of sickness and healing were both conveyed and received have changed. We no longer think of epilepsy, for instance, as being caused by demon possession, any more than we think of the moving of the trees in a strong wind as being the work of shadowy spirits. Our world-view has altered, our thought forms have changed. Just as polytheism gives way to new knowledge of ourselves and our world in terms of pathology, psychology and ecology and the propensity of the mind to unify, so it seems that polydemonism must be discarded in its original and primitive form.

This is not to deny that for most people life is a continual struggle and the Christian has particular kinds of battles to fight against principalities and powers. If we are concerned about original causes rather than symptoms, we may also have to ask questions about national and international policies in regard to health, education, welfare, unemployment, armaments, and other matters that relate to the distribution of resources and the ordering of our world. It is important to see evil in its corporate, as well as in its individual form. A great deal of spiritual warfare is lost or won in the ordinary and everyday arena of life, as well as in the extraordinary and supernatural one.

SIGNS AND WONDERS

One of the remarkable contemporary challenges to Christian churches in the field of healing ministry has been the growth of the 'Signs and Wonders' movement pioneered by John Wimber of the Vineyard Christian Fellowship of Anaheim in North America. The title of the movement derives, of course, from the word in Hebrews: 'It [this salvation] was declared at first by the Lord, and it was attested to us by those who heard him, while God also bore witness by signs and wonders and various miracles and by gifts of the Holy Spirit distributed according to his own will' (Hebrews 2:3–4). John Wimber has spoken of this movement as a means of 'gaining new understanding and growing in ministry skills'. The aim is the laudable one of 'the transformation of the Body of Christ from being an inactive audience to being a Spirit-filled army'. The movement has not been without its critics in Britain and some would regard it as an undesirable, and even dangerous transatlantic import.

Part of the problem of the Signs and Wonders approach to Christian healing is that it too readily equates 'healing' with one particular kind of ministry, namely the charismatic, 'power healing' approach with large, well-publicised gatherings of a particular character, and led by peculiarly gifted leaders with special authority. In so doing, it perhaps also equates too magically the question of healing (curing) and salvation, without sufficiently taking account of the universal phenomena of suffering and death. In fairness to John Wimber, it should perhaps be said that he would not necessarily subscribe to all that is reflected in the attitude of his followers or the public impression given by his special meetings. He remains a humble minister of the gospel, anxious that others should share in the ministry of prayer and healing as they are enabled.

Wimber has described the three great marks of the Kingdom as evangelism, healing and exorcism. One might readily accept the first two of these without being in complete accord about the third. Of course, much will depend upon what we mean by exorcism and how we see it in practice. Surely the Kingdom may be proclaimed in quietness as well as with incantations and confrontations with invisible powers? The work of preaching and healing surely does not require a reversion to medieval superstition. Without denying the need of exorcism under special circumstances and conditions, one would want to place the emphasis in our teaching and healing not upon the bizarre or melodramatic but upon the God who said, 'Let light shine out of darkness', and who has shone in our hearts to give the light of the knowledge of the glory of God in the face of Jesus Christ.[8] Voices are rightly raised in warning against a preoccupation with demonology and exorcism. The late David du Plessis wrote: 'They spend all their time looking for demons – and the devil keeps them so busy looking for him, they don't see the Lord.'[9] He went on to suggest that a lack of discernment in the Church today can arise because Christians fail to recognise that discernment has to do with discerning the mind of the Spirit, and not devils.

It is this in part that makes one wonder whether there is not more than just a touch of Gnosticism (a second-century heresy) in the Signs and Wonders movement. Gnostics denied the ultimate reality and providential goodness of the created world and of human life, and substituted a fanciful world of demon spirits and evil powers. There is more than an echo of this in some of the newer religious movements. Gnosticism also tried to solve the problem of the dual and complementary nature of God in Christ by dividing the Godhead into two and placing the two halves at different levels. In so doing, it altered the nature of God in human experience and service. If Christ was not fully human, as the Gnostics asserted, then God did not completely identify with us in our frailty and suffering and this was a denial of the incarnation. I am sure that it is not in the minds of people like John Wimber to deny the incarnation but to affirm it. However, if the major emphasis in Signs and Wonders ministry is in terms of miraculous physical cure, the casting away of crutches or the exorcising of disease, then there will inevitably grow up a mind that fails to recognise the victory that can come through a serious grappling with unmerited suffering. Whilst Christians should not glorify suffering, they can never evade the fact that Jesus came in fulfilment of the promise in Isaiah of one who in himself would bear our griefs and carry our sorrows.[10] The Christian lives always in thankful awareness of God's grace: 'He who did not spare his own Son but gave him up for us all, will he not also give us all things with him?'[11] But if we are carried away by the triumphalist assurance that, if we come to Christ, we shall know only peace, happiness and deliverance from the uncomfortable things of life, then we may well be disappointed. More seriously, however, we may, howbeit unconsciously, be reducing the incarnation to what we feel it should have been. That way does not lie salvation.

It might also be said that undue emphasis upon Signs and Wonders is a mistake if it becomes a diversion from seeking more obvious ways in which God works. In this respect I recall a comment of Bob Lambourne which gives us all pause for thought. He said: 'I see part of the greatness of a woman as the capacity to care without the pride of curing, and men aren't very good at this.'[12] I seem to recall that Paul had to rebuke the Christians in Corinth for their overweening ambition to perform miracles and speak in tongues. He went on to show them 'a still more excellent way', the way of love. He doesn't deny the spiritual gifts, indeed he urges them earnestly to desire the higher gifts, but not at the expense of love. 'Make love your aim', he says.[13] Christian healing is essentially a function of love. It has to be, since the normative element in Jesus' work of healing was love – love worked out in life. In this way Christian healing is not to be set over against secular healing but has to stand as a reconciling ministry between the sacred and the secular, as a healing to which Christ has brought his sacramental touch.

We should give thanks to God for every sign of renewal within the Christian Church, and we must never by any means seek to quench the divine spark or diminish the working of the Spirit, for in that way we could be saying 'no' to God. In the end, however, the Christian healing ministry will ultimately be judged by whether it moves people forward into faith in God, to mature discipleship, to spiritual and material responsibility, to a living relationship with Jesus Christ, or backwards into primitive superstition and life-denying fear. So we must beware of any form of healing which leaves the sick person apparently 'cured' but less intact, less mature, less whole. It follows that the healing task is never completed by the act of deliverance. We must then proceed to the difficult yet constructive task of enabling that person to become more free from fear, more at home in God's world and better able to 'fight the good fight of faith'.

Finally, it must be clear that Christian healing is not so much concerned with whether a particular system of healing 'works', but with the picture of God and men and women that is reflected in and through any particular theology and practice. One has only to compare the triumphalist approach of some Christian healers and healing movements with the spirituality that lies behind Julian of Norwich's prayer for wounds and sickness, to see the hollowness behind such an approach. Julian prayed for wounds that she might be freed from illusion and brought into unity with the crucified Christ. To suggest, as Julian did, that the 'wounds may be turned into honours' is not to suggest that sickness has any magically purifying effect but that it can focus the mind and heart on what has been chosen as the all-important centre of life – the love of God in Jesus Christ. At the heart of the Church's healing ministry there is always a bringing of the ailing person, the ailing society and the ailing world to this centre – into the presence of the living Lord, so that all sickness may be healed through his will and power to make all things well.

The need for deliverance, both personal and corporate, still remains. How we respond will depend upon how we interpret the conflict between good and evil. We must recognise that there is always the possibility and danger of superstition being concealed within the healing ministry itself. Christianity works by re-creation, and re-creation which is moral rather than magical. Sometimes Christians have been more concerned about miracles of power than miracles of grace, more about renewal of form and function than about renewal of relationship with God and other human beings. We are then thinking of secondary rather than primary concerns.

Let us have our centres of celebration in which we share our joy in God, our hope in Christ and also share the cares and burdens of others. Let us have miracles of renewal, and rituals that are true witnesses to the gospel hope, remembering the part they play in unlocking emotions, in restoring balance, in the development of a Christ-centred life. Let us never forget, however, that our concern is not with semi-magical forms and practices, however effective they may appear to be, but with the fact of Christ crucified and risen from the dead and the redemptive and re-creative power associated with that divine event. Anything less than this is unworthy of our calling and inconsistent with our work for the Kingdom.

Suffering and a God of Love

Rabindranath Tagore, the Indian poet and author, wrote:

> Death belongs to life as birth does.
> The walk is in the raising of the foot
> as in the laying of it down.

In something of the same way, for the Christian to speak of healing is also to speak of suffering, as it is an inescapable part of life. Christians are not exempt from the world's suffering, disease and death, any more than they are from its earthquakes, famines and wars. There is something essentially suspect in our theology if we ever give the impression that by joining the Christian camp people will be specially protected against the hazards, the pain and suffering of life.

Job's questions about suffering and our deserts, and Jesus' comment about the Galileans who had suffered at the hands of Pilate[1] imply that we do not live in a world based purely on a merit system. We are not then to assume that sin and suffering are always causally related. Jesus' subsequent comment on the victims of Pilate's massacre and the need for repentance could be taken, however, to imply that there may be an element of human responsibility, or even sin, underlying a fair measure of the suffering that we experience. The Lockerbie air disaster in December 1988 was not an unforeseeable natural disaster, such as an earthquake, nor was it an act of human error or carelessness. It was, as we now know, the result of an act of human wickedness. It was a terrorist bomb which blew a 747 aeroplane to bits at 31,000 feet and scattered bodies across the Scottish countryside.

It is perhaps wise first of all to acknowledge that human suffering comes from various sources and is of many kinds. It can come in the form of natural disasters, like an earthquake or a hurricane. It can come from accidents that mutilate, disfigure and kill, like air disasters, road or rail collisions. It can come from wars, famines, political oppression and our inhumanity to one another. Suffering may also be due to disease and infections which upset the natural balance upon which we rely for human health. It may come from emotional distress, mental conflict or spiritual torment. In many of these ways, as we shall see later, sin may be involved either directly or indirectly.

As we see and reverence the Creator through his works, we recognise that God is involved in all his creation. Whilst Christians see God as being on the side of health and healing and constantly involved in all the efforts to reduce the suffering due to human accident, disease and sin, they also recognise that all the issues of life and death are contained within God's will and must therefore have eternal meaning. This is not to suggest that God 'sends' suffering as a punishment for sin, although there may well be suffering built in to certain forms of behaviour as a natural outcome of that behaviour. The person who drinks a bottle of whisky a day should not be surprised if he ends up with cirrhosis of the liver, any more than a man who smokes fifty cigarettes a day should be surprised if he eventually develops cancer of the lung. As human beings, endowed with a certain responsibility in God's creation, we are also given a measure of free will and the ability to choose between good and evil. On the other hand, it is clear that suffering is not entirely a matter of human choice or the result of human sin. There is an element of apparent precariousness in human life which means that there is also an element of ambiguity and mystery in human suffering.

Whilst there is no evidence to suggest that God determines that one sparrow shall fall, whilst another flies free, there is always the assurance, 'not one of them will fall to the ground without your Father's will'.[2] This is a world in which dreadful things can happen, but it is God's world, and everything is contained within his purpose. This is something that we find difficult to accept. In its simplest and most direct form the question can be put in the words of Viktor Frankl's six-year-old daughter, who asked: 'Why do we speak of the good Lord?' Her father replied, 'Some weeks ago, you were suffering from measles, and then the good Lord sent you full recovery.' The little girl was not content but retorted, 'Well, but please, Daddy, do not forget: in the first place, he had sent me the measles.' It was an extension of that problem in its more tragic form that caused such anguish to St Augustine and actually kept him back from becoming a Christian for ten years. In almost every kind of suffering there is an element of the ambiguous and the unknown. Few of us who came through the perils of the last world war relatively unscathed, whilst better men and women died or lived to carry the scars, can fail from time to time to wonder at the apparent precariousness of life. It has been said, of course, that suffering is not a problem to be solved but a mystery to be accepted in faith. Yet, as Christianity is a rational faith, we have to keep searching for some kind of understanding. We should recognise, however, that this is an area of life that we can only explore in faith as a great mystery and with great humility.

SUFFERING AND THE PROVIDENCE OF GOD

If we allow that God permits suffering, there is more than a suggestion in the Bible that he abominates it. There can be nothing more unhelpful to people in the midst of the agony of suffering than to be told by someone standing on the sidelines that this is the will of God. The real comfort to people in such circumstances is the assurance that God is in that situation and sharing their sorrow. A Jew who suffered in the Auschwitz concentration camp, speaking on a television programme, *The Light of Experience*, said: 'I believe God was also crying.' The prophet Isaiah echoed this experience when he said of God and his people, 'In all their affliction he was afflicted' and again, speaking of the Suffering Servant, 'Surely he has borne our griefs and carried our sorrows'.[3]

The New Testament carries forward this idea that when we

cry out in pain, we cry to one who knows that pain and shares it with us. In Jesus Christ, God joined us in all the experience of suffering in the most direct, practical and personal way. For Christians, it is this which helps us to make some interpretation of suffering, even though we do not fully understand it. I remember the letter which was sent to me for comment from a Jewish woman whose daughter had been murdered by her boy-friend. The family had tried to persuade their daughter to give up this young man whom they considered unsuitable. The daughter left home to live with him, but came back a few months later. On the fourth day after returning home the man waylaid her on her way back from work and murdered her. The girl's family were overwhelmed by grief and guilt, feeling that perhaps they might have done something to prevent this. They were also troubled by the fact that after their daughter's death they had all prospered in unexpected material ways. The mother wanted to know how this related to divine providence and whether God was making some kind of recompense.

It wasn't until I tried to reply to that letter, taking into account the fact that the family was Jewish and not Christian, that I realised just how much my own theology, though based in Hebrew Scriptures, is shot through with New Testament affirmations about Jesus' suffering and death, and subsequent resurrection and ascension. Without this, where does one begin to find consolation in such a situation without sounding too much like Job's comforters? There is some reassurance, of course, in that beloved twenty-third psalm, 'Even though I walk through the valley of the shadow of death, I fear no evil'. There is the psalmist's cry of faith and hope, 'I believe that I shall see the goodness of the Lord in the land of the living'.[4] There is the somewhat exasperating response of the Book of Job, which provides no intellectual answer to the problem of undeserved suffering, although it leaves the sufferer answered, 'I had heard of thee by the hearing of the ear, but now my eye sees thee . . .'[5] There is that grim story about the daughters of Lot who made their father drunk and seduced him into begetting children by themselves. Of that union Moab was the off-spring.[6] One writer quotes a saying from an ancient Hebrew source: 'Moab is come forth from lust; but Ruth shall come forth from Moab and David from Ruth, and the Messiah from David.' So even that perverse act was somehow brought within the providence of God. We readily take comfort from the fact that God can often make human sin to praise him. But somehow one needs to be able to go on to speak of the fulfilment of the words of the Psalmist and the prophets in Jesus. For the name and nature of Jesus as Saviour can only be glorified when its bearer is carried through the agony of Gethsemane, the cruelty of the Passion, the joy of the Resurrection and the wonder of the Ascension. In this we see God at work in a strange, perplexing and yet ultimately healing way.

THE POWER OF THE PASSION

In the cross we see the love of God, manifested in the woundedness of his Son, becoming the salvation of the world. Here we see suffering, not as the punishment for sin, but as the outcome of conflict with evil in which the innocent bears the pain of the encounter. In that conflict sin is defeated and suffering is transmuted into glory. Here as nowhere else we are able to identify with the cry: 'He was wounded for our transgressions, he was bruised for our iniquities . . . and with his stripes we are healed'.[7] In the overcoming of evil on Calvary and the subsequent events of Easter Day, there rings a note of hope that in their sufferings Christians are involved in a battle in which Christ is engaged with every form of evil and also in the victory which is God's purpose for those who fight the good fight of faith.

As I have already suggested, it is difficult to tell how much one brought up in the religious context of Passion and Resurrection is conditioned to think in such terms and how far the observed experience of life requires this particular thought form. In other words, do the experiences determine the beliefs or does the framework of belief determine the way in which we perceive the experience? In many ways the two are reciprocal. It does seem that in the context of death and resurrection, dying in order to live, we have a paradigm which is both central to any consideration of the practices and doctrinal understanding of Christianity and also to a true understanding of the nature of sin and suffering and to any truly holistic attitude to life.

The problem of suffering, as we have seen, raises questions about the nature of God who wills or permits suffering and, if this suffering is in any way caused by sin, makes a practical response an immediate imperative. The Bible suggests that Jesus went to the cross, not in any self-affirming way, not to achieve the salvation of his own soul, but to declare the loving sovereignty of God over all the principalities and powers of evil. There is another strand in our thinking about the Passion which sees Jesus going to the cross because of his solidarity with, and compassion for, sinful, suffering human beings. His death upon the cross is then seen as a measure of the lengths that he would go rather than abandon his claims on God's love on our behalf. For the central message in Jesus' self-giving is that, in spite of our waywardness and sin, God loves us, and in such a way that the relationship is not to be severed by human sin.

Jesus never trivialised the question of human suffering and sin or offered explanations which made light of human alien-ation and anguish. Instead he took these seriously and attempted to do something about them, by bearing the ultimate cost in himself. If his experience is to be mandatory for us, then those who walk most closely with him will be those who are most sensitive to human hurt and are ready to respond to it most creatively and compassionately.

This means that we recognise that sin, which is the primary cause of Christ's suffering, is also the basis of most human suffering. The meaning of sin may be expressed in terms of the violation of ritual observance, or of legal or moral code, the violation of human potential or of failure to achieve the mark. All of these I see as too individualistic in concept. I lean towards a more corporate definition of sin that has its basis in a breakdown in relationships; between ourselves and God, between ourselves and another, or between ourselves and our environment. There is also a sense in which sin represents a fracture within ourselves, between body and soul, between mind and spirit, a woundedness at the centre of our being.

This, along with the sundering of other relationships, cannot fail to have its physical effect in terms of pain and suffering. Equally, the very context of our lives is often a damaged context and we may both reflect and escalate the woundedness by our own destructive choices, or as the Prayer Book puts it, 'through negligence, through weakness, through our own deliberate fault'.

THE WAY OF COMPASSION

We have also to be prepared to accept that there is a great deal of human suffering for which we can see no explanation and which does appear to be both arbitrary and pointless. This does not mean that we should cease to explore or reflect upon it, or pray for further understanding. The way of compassion must always be not to pretend that we have the answer but to stand with the sufferer, and this may be ourselves, in faithful and loving silence. We are not always very skilful in handling other people's pain. There is always the danger that in our most earnest attempts to be helpful we may in fact be trivialising suffering and doing less than service to the sufferer. I read once of a preacher who, after delivering what he felt to have been a good sermon on the meaning of suffering, was staggered by the comment of one member of the congregation who looked reproachfully at the minister as he left the church and said, 'You've made it worse!'

The most appropriate response to another's suffering, in many situations, may be one of silence. My early association with Compassionate Friends, a self-help organisation for bereaved parents, made me first aware of the fact that thirty thousand children die in Britain every year. Few who have not suffered the agony, and the 'kind of madness', as one bereaved parent put it, which such families endure, can possibly know what this experience really means.

Martin Camroux, a United Reformed Church minister, described the death of his son. Mark David, their first child, was born brain-damaged, because of lack of oxygen in the later stages of delivery. He died after three days. Martin and his wife, Margaret, were deluged by letters, flowers, cakes and offers of help. Martin explained: 'The most help has come from those who haven't tried to tell us anything except that they cared – like the lady who called and said: "We don't know what to say and we don't know what to do", and then handed us a cake. That said it all.' Least helpful were those who tried to give religious advice – like the lady who called and thrust a tract under their noses and made them sit and read it. 'It's interesting,' said the bereaved father, 'that as a general rule the letters which quoted the most texts were those which were the least help. In the moment of loss it's not works you want, it's just support and love.'[8]

So the silence that is required is not a silence of despair but of compassion. This was the tenor of Dietrich Bonhoeffer's comment when hearing of the death of a friend in Poland in 1939. After speaking of the character of the man, a pastor of the Confessing Church, Bonhoeffer went on: 'Where God tears great gaps we should not try to fill them with human words. They should remain open. Our only comfort is the God of the resurrection, the Father of our Lord Jesus Christ, who also was and is his God.'[9]

WOUNDS BECOME HONOURS

There are many who have been helped to bear suffering and loss by companying with the one who bore our griefs and carried our sorrows. St Paul speaks of his great confidence that nothing that happens to him – tribulation, distress or persecution – can separate him from the love of God in Christ Jesus.[10] Julian of Norwich, an anchoress of the fourteenth century, spoke of 'sharing in the wounds of Christ'. She herself prayed for suffering, in order that she might more fully enter into an experience of the Passion of Christ, and so become increasingly a channel of his self-giving love. This prayer was not the outpouring of a diseased mind but represented the longing of a deeply spiritual woman for identification with Christ, growth in the knowledge and love of God, and thus in the healing of others. For salvation, as Julian saw it, included not only eternal destiny but also human healing, fulfilment and delight.

She wrestled with the question of how a God of love could allow such sin and suffering in the world. She was brought to see in her own profound experience of suffering, how human brokenness is met by God's healing love, so that the wounds, whether inflicted by others, or self-inflicted, become the means of discovering healing and wholeness which unsullied innocence or physical well-being could never have known.

Julian described the three medicines for healing or means to salvation as contrition, compassion and longing with the will for God. By contrition she meant a turning from focus on self to focus on God in Jesus Christ. She knew how difficult it is at times to get away from an obsession with our own frailties and sins. We are not to dwell upon these or become too despondent about them. We are to repent promptly, and then lay hold of the love and delight which God has in us.[11] This is contrition. By compassion one is to become identified with the compassionate Christ. When we realise that he has no wish to rebuke and condemn, but rather to help and heal, we can begin to learn how to love ourselves, as a step towards being able to love others. True longing for God is the cornerstone of all the other prayers. It involves single-minded longing, a matter of the will rather than the emotions which are notoriously unreliable. We are not to deny emotion though we may distrust it. True spirituality, however, requires a consistent choice of God and the values of the crucified Christ, whether we feel like it or not. The will itself, as the apostle Paul testified, is not in itself sufficient. It is even at its best divided, reflecting the fragmentation of our being. What is required is the unification of the will, and with it the healing of the emotions. Julian saw this as flowing from a centering on the love of God manifested in the Passion of Christ. This is the integration which Jesus spoke of as purity of heart which enables us to see God. When that much longed-for fulfilment comes then, like Christ, though in a lesser way, we may begin to see our wounds turned into honours. The firm assurance given to Julian is passed on to fellow Christians:

He did not say: 'You will not be troubled, you will not be belaboured, you will not be disquieted'; but he said: 'You will not be overcome.' God wants us to pay attention to these words . . . for he loves us and delights in us, and so he wishes us to love him and delight in him and to trust greatly in him, and all will be well.[12]

HEALING AS RESPONSE

Bob Lambourne once defined healing as 'a satisfactory response to a crisis made by a group of people, both individually and corporately'.[13] The first word to notice is the word 'response'. This is one of the crucial words in any understanding of the gospel of redemption, and also of the healing ministry. The crisis may be a sudden illness, the break-up of a marriage, a redundancy or a bereavement. The key to it all lies in the character of the response, for this determines the quality of the healing. Those who have worked in hospitals, or with sick people at home, will not require that definition to be further unpacked. It is quite clear that the well-being of those who are sick will depend not only upon their own attitude to their illness but also upon the attitude and actions of those around them. The satisfactory response will involve immediate care, compassion and remedial action.

If we carry this definition beyond the individual case, we see that God's solidarity with us in suffering, through Jesus, involves us in a clear commitment to fight against all causes of suffering, actual or potential, in the world. This may mean a battle to see that food and health care are more equally distributed throughout the world. In terms of the present 'green' crisis it will mean doing more to prevent atmospheric and other forms of pollution. Healing in these terms means an immediate response to a crisis, not on the part of the individual, or even of one or two nations, but all nations.

The satisfactory response to one's own crisis may involve a different kind of response: a quiet and humble search for meaning and for adjustment to a different, though possibly a higher, quality of life. Von Hügel said that Christianity does not explain suffering but rather shows us what to do with it. The world is infinitely richer because of the response of those who have allowed their suffering to take them to places unknown to those who have trodden the more untroubled way.

I remember an interview with Dr Patrick Nuttgens in the television programme *Seven Days*. Here Dr Nuttgens spoke of how early on in his life he suffered from poliomyelitis. Then later on came multiple sclerosis. There was, he confessed, a tendency to protest to God but then came the realisation that it was fruitless to protest. When his disability was seen against the disabilities that others suffer, he felt extremely fortunate.

> To assume that God has treated you badly is to see him as a person. He is infinite, eternal. That is to reduce God to our size. This will not do. We are all part of an enormous arena of life, a tiny microcosm. How do we fit into this complex world? The problem is to try to get deeper understanding of all that is going on behind this wonderful world.

Nuttgens confessed that when MS was first diagnosed, he contemplated suicide. Conversation with his wife persuaded him that to think of suicide was appalling selfishness, creating problems for others. But surely he could be allowed to be miserable for twenty-four hours? 'All right,' his wife came back briskly, 'for twenty-four hours, but not a moment longer!' Towards the close of the interview Nuttgens permitted himself this reflection:

> You can live a life of hope even in the middle of appalling disasters. The extraordinary thing is that the world is full of wonderful, absolutely wonderful people, many of them more disabled than I am and yet they are often immensely happy people . . . the even odder thing is that often the sense of love of other people gets greater because you are disabled and I think that goes for many other people too; and so you find yourself part of a huge, hopeful community of people.

When we consider healing as an attribute of response, it is difficult not to think of Gordon Wilson, whose daughter died in his arms as he waited to be dug out from the rubble that engulfed them in the Enniskillen bombing in Northern Ireland. In the *Seven Days* television programme the broken-hearted father captured the sympathy and the compassion of the nation when he said:

> I don't understand, but I bear no ill-will to anybody, nor does my wife. I feel we are getting grace which is helping – very much so! We are supported by the prayers of our friends and our friends themselves . . . I can't understand why I was not taken rather than Marie . . . part of the larger plan. I don't understand that, but . . . I prayed for them [the bombers] last night. I hope I will have the grace to continue to do so.

Here we see clearly that the character of the response determines the quality of the healing that is possible both for the suffering individual and for those around them. I suspect that many who heard Gordon Wilson speak in these terms began to discover a measure of healing of their own inner wounds. For goodness of this kind communicates itself and tends to lift the agony of sin/sickness which troubles most of us for the greater part of our lives.

THE THORN AGAIN – AN OPPORTUNITY FOR GROWTH

When the apostle Paul refers to his thorn in the flesh, he is obviously using a metaphor to describe some deep-seated illness. It was something that constantly reminded him of the frailty of the flesh – the fact that he had a body and that the body can become violently and viciously self-assertive. He describes the illness as 'a messenger of Satan' sent to harass him and keep him human.

Whatever the identity of the thorn in the flesh, Paul thought of it as a 'given' thing; it did not come by chance. If not of divine origin, it was not without divine significance and meaning. Paul saw it as a sort of counterbalance to the 'abundance of revelations' – that he might not be too elated by these ecstatic experiences. So we can say that Paul saw his suffering as sent by Satan and allowed by God, in order to save him from spiritual pride. This enabled him to accept and use the experience, as he saw it was not without its place in the strange economy of God.

Moreover, as Paul tells us in his letter to the Galatians, it was this illness that first brought him to preach the gospel in that city.[14] We are not told just under what circumstances he had turned aside to preach to them, but it was something to do with his sickness and something in and through which he was able to see the hand of God. If he had not preached to them in the first place, there would have been no occasion for him to write to them afterwards. So once again God had over-ruled evil for good.

Paul goes on to insist that it was through his illness that he had been brought to a new understanding of prayer. He prayed three times that the thorn might leave him. He had to learn how to persevere in prayer and at the end of that to discover that God has different ways of answering. He just did not receive any answer to the first two prayers, or not any answer that he could recognise as such. After the third request there was no doubt as to the Lord's reply: 'My grace is sufficient for you, for my power is made perfect in weakness.'[15] God's answer to that prayer was that whilst he would not remove the thorn that was causing the weakness, he would supply power which would be more than sufficient; for this new kind of power, which comes by God's grace is made perfect, finds its full scope, as Knox translates it, in weakness. So those very things which we would most avoid, those things which cause weakness and humiliation, after being taken to the Lord, can actually result in new access of divine strength. Paul could now welcome such experiences in that they had brought him new discoveries of the grace of God and the power of the risen Christ.

I was present some years ago at a conference on Christian healing when two young women from my own church gave their testimony. One had known a miraculous cure of multiple sclerosis ten years previously and since had had no recurrence of her illness. It was a remarkable story which those who heard it will never forget. The other was by a girl who is blind and who declared that she was not looking for a miracle cure of her blindness but had very different aspirations. This was not because she had become resigned to her lack of sight, but because in her blindness she had discovered things about herself, about others and about God that she felt would not have been revealed to her if she had been fully sighted. Of course, if pressed, she might have confessed to an occasional longing to see more of the beauty of the world but not if this meant losing all that God had revealed to her in her blindness. Here was one who had made completely her own what Paul was saying about God's strength being made perfect in weakness.

Another young friend of mine has recently come to the Christian faith. He is 23 and suffers from a devastating degenerative illness which means that he is confined to a wheelchair and daily copes with dreadful limitations and frustrations in a remarkably cheerful way. Indeed his courtesy and good humour shine through and are a challenge to those of us who are more able-bodied. In a recent letter he chatted on about his various activities and friends and then mentioned that he had heard that I was writing a book on Christian healing. Referring to 'healing', he said:

Please don't take this as a personal criticism – but is that the right thing to want? Surely it's up to us to learn to cope, with a bit of help from the Holy Spirit. It would be great if we could cut down on our many problems, but to my way of thinking, there could be the new problem of taking the Lord for granted, if we start to feel that we don't need Him so much. I guess most folk want to lighten their load, but, however hard it may be, I try to accept the obstacles and pitfalls of life as God's will, and thank Him for them.

And then he added characteristically: 'But I try to keep an open mind on the subject of Christian healing, and look forward to reading your book.' Who am I to try to speak about the difference between healing and curing to one who is so manifestly healed?

Michael reveals the shallowness behind the doctrinaire statement of those who earnestly declare that God's will for all of us is perfect health and everything other than that is of the devil. People who speak in those terms remind me of Job's comforters who have not really grappled with the agonies of the situation as Job had. I would rather spend time arguing from the book of Job, or indeed from Jesus and Paul, that all suffering is a challenge to individual and community alike.

Suffering itself, of course, is neutral. It can open new doors and windows into a deeper understanding of ourselves and God, or it can shut us in upon ourselves and produce distorted lives and destructive relationships. Healing comes when suffering is met with the response of faith, hope and love, that is, with God. We should never lose sight of the fact that we are all part of a fallen order, in the process of being redeemed. In that process the response we make to life is critical for ourselves, for those around us, and ultimately for the process of redemption. Our helper in this is the Holy Spirit, the Lord and Giver of Life.

For suffering to be creative and redemptive there has to be a readiness voluntarily to accept, rather than react in anger against, the current situation (to float rather than to fight); an ability to participate in life, even in suffering, and this leads to a higher quality of life; an appreciation of the spiritual element within the very setting of that suffering which seems to preclude it. Many who have entered the darkness of suffering, not expecting there to have a divine encounter, have found God to be there within and around them. So the darkness has been illumined and the way of suffering has become a journey into life with new dimensions.

Some years ago I was invited to minister to a woman who had just been told that her cancer had begun to develop secondaries and her life was being threatened. As she had young children, she became for a time not only anxious but also angry. Healing for her at this stage was seen very much in physical terms. Her family needed her and she slowly learned the importance of just being with them, even if she was unable to do much for them. After numerous spells in hospital and the passing of two years, her attitude began to change so that she could speak of death, even her own death, with some degree of composure. At this time she wrote to me about what a

service of Communion, with laying on of hands, had meant to
her:

> From beginning to end it was reiteration, assurance of the
> promises I have already been given, of the very deep and
> yet hidden belief that I have of being in the process of
> receiving a total healing . . . The actual laying on of hands,
> just as the communion elements, have become very very
> real. I eat and drink Christ's whole (healthy) body and blood
> and claim them instead of my sick ones. Your hands and the
> words of prayer are the symbols, the contact point of God's
> absolute power and love and the reality of his promises . . .
> I still have life in a time context – and He (God) permitted
> the bad to happen when He created us with free will – now
> I believe I see Him sitting on the sidelines, suffering the
> searing agony of watching . . . only able to help at the
> moment when I respond and connect the spirit in me to the
> Spirit in Him – from then on He is right in the whole agony
> with me . . .
> He was with me in the depths of despair and tears when I
> wondered through the pain if I'd ever get home again. He
> was with me in the high bits when nothing mattered but God
> – and in the middle bits when I was out of pain and longing
> only for the family and home.
> And through it all, strengthened by each laying on of
> hands . . . has been this quiet assurance of healing.

This dear friend of mine died just twelve months after writing
that letter, but not before she had witnessed gloriously to the
fact that Christian wholeness is more, much more than physical
completeness. Those who are disciples of Jesus Christ should
know this all too well. The torn flesh and gaping wounds seen
on Calvary should help us to dispose of that view of wholeness
which consists in perfection of shape and form.

Christ's victory on the cross has been variously interpreted
but it represents for me the sublime and, I hope, not shallow
optimism, that given the Christlike response to suffering and
death, in the end all manner of things shall be well. It suggests
that this mortal crucible is finally creative and not just a tor-

menting fire; that the painful experiences of life do not go for nothing but add up to something special. Whether we can describe that something as resurrection depends upon how close we can get to Christ's obedience, his faithfulness and his self-denying love.

Healing and the Local Church

Dr Lesslie Newbigin tells of the time when, as Director of World Mission and Evangelism for the World Council of Churches, he was almost overwhelmed by the total inadequacy of mission resources to meet the medical needs of developing countries. He spoke about his concern for mission hospitals to Dr G. Adeyemi Ademola, a Nigerian doctor who was representing his government. Dr Ademola listened carefully, there was a long silence, then he said: 'But, of course, the primary agency of healing is the local congregation.' This was in the 1960s when technology was everything and Newbigin confesses that this was for him a completely new insight. That comment was an important factor in the thinking of the Tübingen consultation which led to the report 'The Healing Church'.[1]

Underlying the comment of that Nigerian doctor was a worldview very different from our western secular view of life and health and one much closer to that of the New Testament where healing was seen as the overcoming of the powers of evil by the power of the living Christ. In that view, healing and preaching go together as two sides of the same coin. The healing authenticates the preaching and both are instruments of the kingly rule of God.

DIFFICULTIES IN SEEING THE CONGREGATION AS A PRIMARY AGENCY OF HEALING

To suggest to a Christian congregation today that it is called to be the primary agency of healing would be to invite a response of confusion and dismay. There are various reasons for this. One may be because we have too often lost a real sense of the congregation as a worshipping community with a corporate and missionary responsibility to discharge before God. All too often congregations come together in a random sort of way to worship without any real sense of being the Church of God, in which common loyalties are accepted, mutual understanding is sought, various tasks are performed and regular worship is offered, all under the rule and continuing ministry of the Risen Christ. That is a terrible loss to any Christian community's sense of identity, purpose and continuing worth.

There is also the not inconsiderable fact that within the western world the minority status of the active Christian is becoming more and more apparent. Already it is being demonstrated that, whatever organisations like Christian Aid and the World Council of Churches can do, the problems of racialism, poverty and the destructive power of unredeemed humanity are likely to make the specifically Christian contribution rather like the widow's mite. This need not daunt us if, as with Mother Teresa of Calcutta, our theology is secure. When challenged about the marginal nature of the relief that she and her nuns are able to bring to the sufferings of that vast subcontinent of India, Mother Teresa replies with breath-taking simplicity: 'We ourselves feel that what we are doing is a drop in the ocean. But if that drop was not in the ocean I think the ocean would be less because of that missing drop.'[2] Here is a modern saint who refuses to get lost in numbers but sees that what matters in the Kingdom is to show love and respect for the one person who is before her as the living Christ. If the labourers are few, the harvest is large and the resources are unlimited.

Another of our difficulties in seeing the local church as a healing community is that we know ourselves too well. We know that we are unhealed and so unlike what is required if we are to offer ourselves as a living expression of the love of God in Jesus Christ. Some would say that we must first ourselves be healed if we are to help others to healing. But is this not perhaps to be too idealistic? One of the characteristics of Alcoholics Anonymous is that its members are ready to accept that they are not well, that their only hope is in God and in one another. If we were able to take a similar stance, we might be at once more compassionate towards others and of more service to them. We might also discover in the process that we ourselves were being healed.

Then again, because of the complexity of modern society and greater specialisation of function, the place of the local congregation in healing is assumed, not unnaturally, to be diminished. So the local doctors, the local hospitals, health centres and outworkings of the NHS are seen as the principal agents of healing. We ought positively to affirm all that medicine is doing today and give massive thanks to God for all the gifts that he has given into human hands for the prevention and cure of disease. But we can do this whilst at the same time recognising that because of its success, medicine has in some ways become isolated from other areas of life. This has now reached the point where people see more and more of their needs in medical terms. This leads to increasing pressure being put upon medical resources and medical people. Eventually expectations become so widespread that the doctor becomes the priest, pills take the place of the sacramental bread and wine, salvation comes to be seen in medical terms, and we end up with an idolatry of health. Health, thus robbed of its wider context, is seen in secular terms and a whole dimension of life is lost. The local church and the Christian gospel are written off, even by members of the Church, as an agency of community care and healing. The dethroning of the powers of evil, of which sickness is a characteristic expression, then becomes a function of the State, regardless of the fact that the State may be under the influence of those same powers.

The essentially tragic nature of this development is seen perhaps more clearly when we look at our attitude to death and bereavement. Is it true perhaps that western society today does not really know what to make of death? Christians themselves sometimes forget that the great deliverance which the early Christians saw in their faith was that it brought salvation from the twin powers of sin and death. In the death and resurrection of Jesus, death was seen to be swallowed up in victory:

Lives again our glorious King:
Where, O death, is now thy sting?

I shall describe later on the way in which one church community, sustained by the divine promises about Christ's victory
over death, experienced Christ's healing power at work in a
remarkable way. To lose that area of spirituality from our
community life would be to increase rather than diminish the
sickness in society.

THE EARLY CHURCH

All this makes it important that we should look again at the
characteristic concepts of the New Testament Church, which
incidentally were very similar to those followed by early medical missions, where healing was seen as involving a dethroning
of the powers of evil by the powers of the Kingdom of God.
In the main this dimension of spirituality has largely disappeared from the consideration of the western Church, as being
a scarcely appropriate or relevant way of approach for a Christian of today. Do we perhaps need to look more carefully at
this? What do we mean by demonic powers? How are these
related to sickness? Is it true that the twentieth-century equival-
ent of the early signs and wonders takes place rather less in
our churches than in our hospitals, laboratories, special clinics
and even legislative assemblies? These are all questions that I
have touched on elsewhere in this book. They are questions
that any lively congregation might seriously consider if they are
to recover their true sense of being a primary agency of healing.

The early Christians believed themselves called by Jesus to
restore the suffering, the lost and those borne down by sin,
and demonstrated a remarkable capacity to do so. After Pente-
cost we are told: 'They went forth and preached everywhere,
while the Lord worked with them and confirmed the message
by the signs that attended it.'[3] In his account of the healing of
the lame man at the Beautiful Gate of the temple, Peter
declares: 'The faith which is through Jesus has given the man
this perfect health in the presence of you all.'[4] Luke records:

'Now many signs and wonders were done among the people by
the hands of the apostles.'[5] He goes on to tell how the sick
were carried out into the streets, and laid on beds 'that as Peter
came by at least his shadow might fall on some of them', that
they might be healed.[6] The time came when emphasis upon
healing cures gave way to an encouragement to bear patiently
with illness and to regard it as a way by which Christians might
share in the wounds of Christ.

The vital message that came through the early preaching and
living, however, was 'God has visited his people'.[7] This visi-
tation provoked both joy and awe, and an amazing confidence.
Those early Christians were given the assurance that through
their membership of the Christian community they were heirs
of a spiritual kingdom in which healing energies were at work
beyond their capacity to understand them. The three cardinal
virtues, which St Paul recognised in Jesus' ministry and saw
carried to supreme heights on Calvary, were faith, hope and
love. These were the keys to this new kingdom. In healing
terms this meant, in general, faith on the part of the patient
and, in particular, love on the part of the healer. Love was the
essential characteristic behind Jesus' ministry of healing. Hope
was a quality shared by both patient and healer alike, and it
was not just a vague wishful thinking but, as Von Hügel put
it, 'eager tiptoe expectancy', alert and ready to act. Always it
was a response to love, God's love to us in Jesus but also the
expression of that love worked out in life and under the influence of the Holy Spirit. So a vital faith encouraged a vital
church and this produced a vital religion.

A CONTINUING CHALLENGE TO THE CHURCH TODAY

We may be living in a new age but the historic commission and
promises remain. The Kingdom of God has been revealed. In
Christ's incarnation, life, death and resurrection the forces of
evil have been dethroned. If shadowy figures are still around
in dark corners, God has provided a way of deliverance and
the Church has ways of continuing the battle. It does this, as
the Early Church did, by preaching the Word, by celebrating

the sacraments and by its common life and work. Perhaps it is worthwhile reaffirming what the Church is doing today. By its public worship and its less public support of individuals who are facing suffering with courage and constancy, by its programmes of relief and institutions of care, the Church is healing. During the last twenty years there has also been a much greater take-up of healing ministry in terms of the introduction of special services for healing. But this is not the only, or perhaps even the main, criterion upon which one might judge the Church's healing role.

True healing is always a demonstration of that total victory which Jesus accomplished by his death and resurrection, but it is a demonstration anchored in human life. So our conception of healing must be broad enough to include the work done in our hospitals and health centres, in the evangelistic outreach of the Church, in the work of technological assistance in developing countries, in the healing of relationships between peoples of different racial origin, between Catholic and Protestant, between Christian and Muslim and so on. Nothing else will do because nothing else will adequately reflect the wonder of God's love for all people and his will that they be made whole.

What is increasingly clear is that it is not sufficient to offer prayer for someone suffering from the 'demons' of loneliness, malnutrition and general neglect without doing something to provide a balanced diet, reasonable living conditions and occasional company. This is true of so many of the complex and widespread problems from which individuals suffer as a result of being members of a discordant, selfish and divided society. Only very slowly and painfully do we learn that people discover their wholeness, not in isolation but in community.

In Chelmsford, where I ministered from 1973 to 1984, we had a modern building with splendid facilities. This enabled us to run a number of activities involving people in the community. Church members found themselves involved with others in luncheon clubs, a work-centre for retirement pensioners, a play-group for children, a weekly meeting for people suffering from depression, and various other organisations and groups, including later a work-centre for the unemployed. In all this, together with pastoral work, weekly chapel prayers, the Sunday services and the regular services for healing, members of the congregation were encouraged to see themselves as part of a pattern of healing activities in which Christ was present in his church.

In my present part-time ministry in St Ives I have seen how the congregation as a whole has reacted in loving faith to a terrible car accident in which three young people were killed and one suffered severe head injuries. The church was, of course, devastated by this loss. What was remarkable about the next few days and weeks was the way in which the bereaved and suffering parents, together with their friends in the congregation, and not least the young people, comforted and cared for one another in a remarkably healing way. In this, ministers and people recognised their vulnerability and need of one another and were ready to share in a personal and self-giving way. The reality of death intensified the reality of Christ's presence in our common life.

As a result of that experience of suffering and loss, but also in response to a general desire to understand more fully the healing ministry of the church, a working party was set up. This followed a church weekend during which we looked together at healing as an aspect of spirituality. The group included a local GP who is a member of the church, one of the ministers and other members of the congregation. Our task was to examine the possibility of developing the healing ministry in the church. After some months of prayer and preparation and general agreement by Elders and Church Meeting, healing services have been introduced and we have the assurance that they are integral to our common life of prayer and praise and not just grafted on to a lifeless body.

When considering the healing ministry of the local church it is important to ensure that the members of the church have some understanding of the wider context of healing and its underlying philosophy, and also of the relationship of the church to the community in which it is set. The concept of healing in terms of the eradication of defects is still deeply fixed in many people's minds.

RESOURCES – BUILDINGS

It is also important that we take a careful, indeed critical, look at our resources. Most churches are all too painfully aware that they have buildings. We tend to see these as liabilities which are simply an enormous financial drain upon resources, rather than in themselves a resource which can be used in the development of the church's ministry. Many years ago George Bernard Shaw wrote:

> If some enterprising clergyman with a cure of souls in the slums were to hoist a board over his church door with the following inscription: .
>> 'Here men and women after working hours may dance without getting drunk on Friday, hear good music on Saturdays, pray on Sundays, discuss public affairs without molestation by the police on Mondays; have the building for any honest purpose they choose on Tuesdays; bring the children for games, amusing drill and romps on Wednesdays; and volunteer for a thorough scrubbing down of the place on Thursdays',
>
> he could reform the whole neighbourhood.

The expression of the idea may be somewhat dated, but the idea is essentially sound – and sound not only in terms of 'reforming' the neighbourhood but also in bringing healing and renewal to both church and community.

During a visit to Kingston, Jamaica, a couple of years ago, I was impressed by the way in which Meadowbrook Church found ways of reaching out into the community. The church is set cheek by jowl with one of the city's shanty towns. Apparently there is no national provision for nursery education. Those living in that part of Kingston would not be able to afford private nurseries. The church has good buildings and within the church complex runs a secondary school, but they have no room for nursery classes. Rather ingeniously, I thought, they bought very cheaply two old single-decker British Leyland buses, placed them on a spare bit of ground across from the church and set up nursery classes in them.

As we were shown round the main church premises, we entered one room equipped as a doctor's surgery and another with a dentist's chair. Apparently a local doctor and dentist, members of the church, give time each week to bring relief to members of the local community who would not be able to meet professional fees. In the same way a solicitor and account-ant give professional advice for a period each week as part of their stewardship of the gospel. The day we visited there was a display of garments produced by unemployed teen-age girls who had just completed a six-week course in dressmaking spon-sored and provided by the church. In this way the church uses its buildings and personnel as an expression of the gospel requirement to heal, to care and to save.

RESOURCES – PEOPLE AND RELATIONSHIPS

It is now more generally recognised that sickness and health are in part an expression and result of the interaction between individuals and between individuals and their environment.

One of the things we noticed early on in our time in Chelms-ford was the number of very lonely people about, and not just amongst the older members of the community. Many people depended upon the church for an important part of their com-munity life. Drivers of the church mini-bus reported that if for some reason any of the older people were unable to get to the Day Centre for a week or two, especially if they lived on their own, there was a noticeable decline in their general sense of well-being. It was the stimulus of having to get ready to go out, and in the meeting with others, that the deteriorating effects of ageing were kept at bay. Over two hundred meals a week were prepared and cooked on the church premises to supply the needs of the Day Centre – all by voluntary helpers and many of them pensioners. The woman who organised all this, herself a volunteer, just refused to have a washing-up machine or an automatic potato peeler in the kitchen, on the grounds that they would take away jobs that some of the helpers did and found satisfaction in being able to do. So we learned that people we have in our churches, who are willing and able to serve in community-based activities, are an important resource in the church's healing ministry. Here also it is seen that healing in these terms is not the prerogative of any one group or profession. It lies within the competence of ordinary people who, seeing a need, give themselves whole-heartedly, find themselves being equipped to meet it, and discover to their surprise and joy that in the process they are themselves being healed.

We shouldn't really be surprised about this. Gerald Caplan tells how he was present at a meeting with a group of psychiatrists where Dr Lilley of Bethesda was talking about his research. He came home very excited about the meeting to be met by his daughter, aged thirteen. She asked where he had been. He told her. She wanted to know what it had been all about. He described experiments in isolating people from community and the effects it had on them. His daughter replied pertly, as only a thirteen-year-old can, 'You psychiatrists, you're always finding out things that everyone knows.' He asked her what she meant. 'Well,' she answered, 'everyone knows that isolation produces mental disorder. Look at Treasure Island, look at Ben Gunn, he was marooned on the island and didn't he go crazy, and look at all the prisoners they put in dungeons, and don't they go crazy?' Caplan had to admit that his daughter was right.[8] He went on to list the interpersonal requisites for mental health: the need for love, for support, for impulse control, the need to feel part of a group, for personal achievement and recognition. All these needs have to be satisfied to a greater or lesser degree if people are to achieve any kind of wholeness. Undoubtedly the family supplies many of these needs but there are many people who, for one reason or another, do not have families with whom they can interact in this way. Then the relationships provided in a church community are very important.

We must also recognise that in a mature and healing community there is an element of mutuality in relationships. The healing comes in both giving and receiving. There is no one person or group of people who do the giving and another person or group who do the receiving. That was part of the difficulty with the old idea of missionary activity. We did the sending, others did the receiving and we tended to be rather proud that it was this way round. We have now come to a more satisfactory sense of mission being a two-way process. In his essay, 'The Gift', Marcel Mauss, explores this topic of gift-exchange among the Polynesians and the Amerindians, and shows the value of their custom whereby no one gave without receiving or could receive without giving. The community life of such societies was ordered through a careful pattern of offerings and counter-offerings, so that, by implication, no goods belonged entirely to one person or group. Edwin Muir puts this same idea in one of his poems:

> This that I give and take,
> This that I keep and break,
> Is and is not my own
> But lives in itself alone
> Yet is between us two.

Paul suggests much the same thing about the Church as the Body of Christ: 'The eye cannot say to the hand, "I have no need of you," nor again the head to the feet, "I have no need of you." '9

The exciting thing about many of our more progressive churches today is that they have learned, or are rapidly learning, the art of gift exchange – of one person giving to another and receiving from another. This partnership in a common task not only preserves the personal dignity of all involved but also draws out unsuspected gifts and talents which might otherwise remain undiscovered. There must always be a partnership in a common task, a true sharing in pastoral care and mutual self-giving, if we are to be part of that multiplication of love for which in Adam we were made and to which in Christ we are miraculously restored.

In trying to provide a sense of physical community for those who are lonely or ill at ease, we should never forget the spiritual loneliness people feel by their sense of personal alienation from God and from all that is good. I cannot forget the look on the face of a woman who came to me at the end of a meeting and said: 'You may not believe this, but I have spent the last thirty-

five years trying to convince myself that I was not a nuisance
to myself and to everyone else.' Would that we could see that
all our church groups, whatever their apparent purpose, had
this inner one of sharing fellowship and study, in order that
repentance, confession and realisation of forgiveness and healing might be worked at together.

RESOURCES – THE GOSPEL

We do well to remember that amongst the resources that are
available to us are not only buildings and people but also the
gospel, with its ability to provide what Harry Emerson Fosdick
once described as 'the expulsive power of a new affection'.
Here is a dynamic that is distinctively our own, if only we are
prepared to own and possess it. The great ones in the Christian
tradition have always seen the world's healing coming through
the small company of the faithful, the remnant, whose form
is most clearly seen in the one who was wounded for our
transgressions. When his arms were spread wide upon the cross,
he revealed the greatest instrument of healing the world will
ever know. For God was then in Christ reconciling the world
to himself. When that sublime, prophetic act was accomplished
and Christ returned to his disciples in risen form, he passed on
to them the healing charge and the reconciling power. He did
not ask them to take political power or to build a spiritual
empire but simply to preach, teach and to heal. They were to
'heal the sick, cleanse lepers, raise the dead, cast out demons'.
In their day they did. We may interpret our task differently
today, but in form only, not in substance. In his novel, *Angel
Pavement*, J. B. Priestley says of one of his characters, 'He
lived in a world from which gods had been banished, but not
the devils.' In that he was perhaps speaking to our condition
today.

During my ministry in Coventry, I came to know Jimmie, a
sporadic member of the church youth group. Jimmie was a
loner, rather older than the others, unemployed and he had a
drug problem. He also had a background of deprivation and
rejection. I found him one night sitting in a corner of an upstairs

corridor at the church weeping because he felt the other young-sters were rejecting him. Some weeks later I was called out late at night to visit his bed-sit where I discovered that he was gently slicing his wrists. I went with him to the hospital and kept in touch for some time afterwards. The next I heard was that he had been sent by a member of the Probation Service to a farm community in Gloucestershire where Christian workers operated a drug rehabilitation centre. Some six months later, one of our students in London telephoned to say that the previous Sunday he had visited Duke Street Baptist Church in Richmond where ten young men received Christian baptism. One of them he thought he recognised. When the names were read out, he knew it was indeed Jimmie, who had been with us in Coventry. A week or so later Jimmie came back to see us and to confirm that, though he still had problems, he had discovered the healing power of the gospel.

One way of estimating the health of the local congregation might be by an examination of the way it holds together and uses creatively its major resources in a complete and continuing worship of the God and Father of our Lord Jesus Christ. This is not something that we can achieve ourselves. This kind of integration and application can come only under the inspiration and guidance of the Holy Spirit. Writing about evangelism in the city, Lesslie Newbigin said:

> How can this strange story of God made man, of a crucified saviour, of resurrection and new creation become credible for those whose entire mental training has conditioned them to believe that the real world is the world that can be satisfac-torily explained and managed without the hypothesis of God? I know of only one real hermeneutic of the gospel: a congre-gation which believes it.

He goes on to suggest that evangelism is not just a matter of techniques or winning people to our way of thinking. There is always the telling of good news, but what really changes people's hearts and converts their wills is a mysterious working of the Holy Spirit and we are not permitted to know more than a little of his secret working. 'But – and this is the point – the

Holy Spirit is present in the believing congregation gathered
for praise and the offering up of spiritual sacrifice, scattered
throughout the community to bear the love of God into every
secular happening and meeting. It is they who scatter the seeds
of hope around . . .'[10]

HEALING OUR RELATIONSHIPS

Paul Tournier described relationships as the 'third dimension
of medicine'. Jesus described them as the first dimension of
religion: 'You shall love the Lord, your God . . . and your
neighbour as yourself.'[11]

We are not, however, always very successful in handling
relationships, even within our churches. What constitutes a
healthy and health-giving relationship may depend more than
we know upon a satisfactory response to that twin command:
'You shall love the Lord . . . and your neighbour . . .' This
sets us three immediate questions. What do we mean by love?
What do we mean by loving our neighbour as ourselves? Finally, what is the relationship between these two questions and
the revelation of God's love in Jesus Christ?

Love, of course, is a word that has been diminished by
current use. In this context it means more than warm affection.
A useful starting point might be with the word 'acceptance' –
not in a mean or grudging way but more in the sense of respect
or 'positive regard' – a recognition that we can accept one
another as expressions of the living activity of the living God.
We might then understand that unity of spirit does not mean
uniformity of interests, attitudes, viewpoints and tempera-
ments. Much distress and brokenness of spirit might be avoided
if we could accept one another in all our limitations and forgive
one another as we hope to be forgiven. Loving our neighbour
'as ourselves' must in any straightforward interpretation mean
doing to them as we would have them do to us. But there is
perhaps also the implication that we shall be unable to love
others fully unless we have learned to love ourselves. It does
seem that many people are so basically unhappy with themselves, so unready to respond to God's love for them, that

they are unable to love anyone else. This is where personal confession and restoration of relationship with God may be good not only for the individual soul but also for the corporate body, the community itself. Our love can never be what it should be until it becomes like that self-giving, all-embracing love that was seen in Jesus on Calvary. 'In this is love, not that we loved God but that he loved us and sent his Son to be the expiation for our sins.'[12] True love always carries within it this readiness to sacrifice for the loved one. If our relationships were characterised by this kind of love then we might be able to love the unlovely, to criticise with kindness and praise without patronising. We might also be able to do the best things in the best way – a way that is creative rather than destructive. To give relationships the priority they deserve is also to serve the cause of Christian healing.

We know what we are; we do not yet know what we shall be, if 'ransomed, healed, restored, forgiven', we are enabled by God's Holy Spirit to be made completely whole and entirely his. The local congregation, however small and weak, when it accepts this kind of calling, can become a true source and centre of healing.

Healing Prayer

It is recorded of the Early Church: 'They met constantly to hear the apostles teach, and to share the common life, to break bread, and to pray. A sense of awe was everywhere, and many marvels and signs were brought about by the apostles.'[1] Whether or not there was a simple correlation between prayer and signs and wonders, it is almost certainly true that there was a direct link between prayer and the character of that Christian community. The teaching, breaking of bread and prayer were elements that held together their common life and from that common life there came 'many marvels and signs'. We know now that prayer is central to the work of healing, in so far as healing means more than the healing of symptoms but the discovery of wholeness, harmony and fulfilment.

William Temple, one of the most distinguished and widely loved Archbishops to occupy the See of Canterbury in this century, was one of the busiest and most brilliant men of his day. Temple held that prayer is the chief thing in the Christian life. Professor Hodgson, who knew him well, traced the source of his patience and graciousness of mind to the inner life of prayer. He tells how, after a stormy meeting, Temple led the delegates into chapel for closing prayers:

As he opened the Bible and began to read the whole atmosphere was changed. There was no mistaking the fact that we were being lifted up to the realm where he habitually dwelt. We knew then whence came the courtesy, the patience, the love of justice and the calm strength with which he had led us into order out of the chaos of our controversies.

Some of the greatest spiritual guides, as well as the most effective agents of healing power, have been men and women of prayer. Because their souls were sustained by a disciplined stillness and quiet waiting upon God they were able to bring guidance and healing to others.

Without denying delight in the sudden event – the falling in love, the discovery of joy, the moment of wonder – we must also recognise that many of the greatest experiences in the Christian life come gradually, rather than in an instant. We have already noted that healing, when properly understood, is best seen as a process rather than a single event. Prayer is another of those gifts of God that reaches its finest expression when seen as a process rather than an emergency response to a critical event. This is true of petition and intercession but it is particularly true of two forms of prayer which are often neglected where healing is concerned: adoration and confession.

ADORATION

At the heart of Christian prayer is communion, something deeper than communication, more demanding but also ultimately more rewarding than just 'saying our prayers'. In our personal prayer, the prayer of adoration must have a special, if not central, place. It takes courage and inner confidence to venture along this road of inner silence, quiet contemplation and adoration. Most will probably need some help in focusing attention in order to make the most of these moments of perception. Some may find a candle, an icon or a cross a help to drawing near to God in this way. The aim is to move from the head to the heart: into the area of feeling, sensing, listening and loving. There are obvious dangers in living too much in the head. One is that we live too much in the past, regretting past follies, recalling past injuries. The other is that we live too much in the future, dreading future possibilities and events. This all leads to increasing tension, rather than relaxation and renewal. The movement from the head to the heart means that we learn to live in the present and also to live more completely in the life of God.

Dr J. S. Whale, urging students at Cambridge to follow Luther's advice and go beyond studying the commands of God to the act of listening to God commanding, said:

> Instead of putting off our shoes from our feet because the place whereon we stand is holy ground, we are taking nice photographs of the burning bush from suitable angles, chatting about theories of the atonement with our feet on the mantelpiece, instead of kneeling down before the wounds of Christ.

I suspect it is not only theological students who need to hear that counsel about kneeling down before the wounds of Christ. We also need to take seriously the suggestion of restoring the contemplative element in spirituality. We lose so much because we have surrendered the ability to 'be still and know'. Much growth might come if we were more ready to say with Jesus, 'Abba, Father', and cultivate that deep silence in which God is known and we are able to see more clearly 'the light of the knowledge of the glory of God in the face of Jesus Christ'.

CONFESSION

We often say that confession is good for the soul; we do not always appreciate that it is good for both soul and body. For this reason, as well as for others, it is perhaps unfortunate that confession has often been seen too much in terms of the Catholic rite of 'making my confession', with all that that suggests of priestcraft and even, perhaps, a certain kind of permissiveness. A good starting point for confession might well be the abandonment of the desire to be always right. I listened recently with interest to a high-powered and wealthy businessman talking about his business. He said that when at meetings with his staff one of them would assure him that he was right, he would reply, 'I am not interested in being right, I *am* interested in being rich.' Fortunately he was able to say that with a smile and a twinkle! It suggested to me that Christians ought to be sufficiently secure in their faith to be ready to abandon the desire to be right, if only they might be rich before God.

True penitence lies at the heart of all Christian life and service. We should never underestimate its importance in the process of Christian healing. That is surely why the Jesus Prayer – 'Lord Jesus Christ have mercy on me' – is so important in cleansing the mind and heart of its sickness. Confession is not so much a morbid searching out of our faults, but rather an honest acknowledgement to God of *what* we are – sinners in need of grace – and *where* we are on our Christian journey. It is a putting away of pretence, even self-pretence and especially self-deceit. It is a healthy admission before God: 'Yes, this is me. I am like this.' It is a recognition that God already knows us better than we know ourselves ('from whom no secrets are hidden'). It reflects what is almost a pressure from God to accept ourselves for what we are, as God also accepts us in his love. It may lead on to the entirely proper and formal act of confession. True confession, however, does not consist in just reciting a laundry-list of our infidelities. It is more inward than that and involves a recognition of sin, the sin which brought Jesus to the cross, which is the source of so much human suffering and which lies at the centre of our own pain and brokenness. This is not to trivialise 'sins' but to see them for what they are: as symptoms of a greater problem, namely our alienation from God and the disintegration of human personality. Unless some relief is provided from the resultant mental and spiritual anguish, we become snarled up in internal struggles from which guilt, alienation and a sense of worthlessness eventually erupt into even more damaging behaviour to ourselves and others. This is so unnecessary, for God has already provided a way of redemption and reconciliation in his Son. It is for the Church to make real the possibility of renunciation of sin and enable true repentance and healing to take place. The Church has such medicines available and her teaching about the need for penitence and the practice of the prayer of confession are foremost amongst these. It behoves the Church, due confession and amendment of life having been made, to encourage people not to stay with those sins but to move on to rejoice in God's goodness and delight in his love. In all this, individual counselling will have an important part to play in the realisation of forgiveness and the achievement of healing.

HEALING AND THE SACRAMENTS

Christians will begin with the conviction that the whole of the Church's life and worship is an expression of its healing ministry, in so far as it reflects God's love and power in Jesus Christ under the guidance of the Holy Spirit. In this the sacraments of baptism and Holy Communion are powerful means of grace. They are more than just symbolic acts, in that they do something. They convey what they mean, namely the essential truth of our redemption in Jesus Christ.[2] It is in the quiet and faithful use of these sacraments and the teaching that underlies them that many will have come to feel and know the healing power of Christ. I do not intend here to enlarge on the sacrament of baptism, though there will be many who have found in this rite Christ and his grace present and powerful to bless, to heal and to save. Baptism is unrepeatable, and the source of much discussion at the present time. There are, however, other acts and rites which are sacramental in nature in that, by the use of signs and symbols, spiritual truth is conveyed and grace is made real to the believer. I shall turn to these later.

HOLY COMMUNION OR THE LORD'S SUPPER

The Reformed theologian, P. T. Forsyth, once said that sacraments are necessary for the health of the Church. For many the Communion service is *the* service of healing. It is a making of Christ and his grace present, the offering of reconciliation where there has been alienation, and through the restored unity, healing of body, mind and spirit.

Some indication of the relationship between sacrament and healing may be seen by considering the essential characteristics of the service. It is an observance carried out in obedience to our Lord's injunction to his disciples, 'Do this in remembrance of me'. He went on to speak of his body given for us and his blood poured out for us. So it is a eucharist, a giving thanks for what God has done for us in offering new life to us in his Son. It is the great confessional act of the Church in which we recall not just our sins but also our faith in what God has done to meet our condition. It is also an act of communion, and it was a wise instinct that connected with this sacrament the 'Comfortable Words', 'Come to me, all who labour and are heavy laden, and I will give you rest'. For here we can share some of the impossible burdens we have been trying to carry on our own, with the one who alone can give us rest. We also renew our sense of community with one another in the Christian fellowship. In this service we are reminded of Jesus' word about the cup as 'the new covenant in my blood'. What we receive in the sacrament is the total gift of Christ himself, as new creation. What is required of us is a total response in faith – the renewal of our covenant with Christ. Having renewed that covenant, having given up ourselves to the Lord and to one another, we are then commissioned by Christ and sent out: 'Go in peace and serve the Lord.'

Nowhere more effectively than in the sacrament of Communion are Christians brought more clearly to the point where two worlds meet, the fallen world and the world of the Kingdom. Here, through Christ, the fallen world is directed towards justification, redemption and renewal. Here also the world of the Kingdom is seen as a present possibility. By the help of the Holy Spirit, as we share in the broken bread and poured-out wine, we also share in that direction and deliverance and in the possibilities of the healed and healing Kingdom.

As in the Early Church the gospel suffered from the distorting influence of the mystery religions, so today the healing ministry is not unaffected by ideas which derive from magical rather than biblical concepts. We do well to remember that what is given to us in the sacrament is power not powers: grace and mercy from the practice of a moral and spiritual faith, and not gifts through rites based upon magical concepts of power. If we are able to keep in mind these central ideas of the sacrament – obedience, thanksgiving, confession, communion, covenant and commissioning – then our ministry of healing can be saved from distorting and divergent influences.

THE LAYING ON OF HANDS

The laying on of hands in biblical times was occasionally used as an act of commissioning, in which a person was separated for a particular work. It was also seen as a powerful symbol of blessing and healing. We know that with a healing word, Jesus would sometimes lay his hands on people as a sign of his care and with the intention of healing. When used in a service today, it should be seen as an act of the Church. Whoever offers the laying on of hands does so in the name of Christ and as a representative of the Church. There are obviously differences of practice if we are involved in a public service as opposed to private ministry. In either case there are no hard and fast rules of procedure. The most that we can do is offer guide-lines. If it is to be a formal and public service it is important that careful consultation and preparation are made beforehand and that arrangements are provided for pastoral follow-up afterwards.

Without denying the value of quiet informal ministry in the home, one can say that the act of laying on of hands is probably at its best when set within the context of a worshipping community, meeting in the name of Christ and open to the empowering of the Holy Spirit. It may or may not be within the context of a communion service. It should be surrounded by prayer and praise, firmly based upon the Word of God and preceded by careful teaching which makes clear that we are not just looking for physical cure. In all the recorded instances in the New Testament where Jesus and the disciples laid hands on people for healing, there appears to be a direct link between action and recovery – something happened, a new factor had entered into the situation. This sometimes makes people today disappointed if there are not immediate signs of physical cure following such a service. There is a need to deal with such expectations in a careful and sensitive way. Thomas Aquinas said, 'Grace flows from the soul to the body.' We have to be prepared for the fact that gradualness is often God's way and the physical is often the last area of life in which healing takes place. Even so, the British Medical Journal suggested some years ago: 'There is no tissue of the human body wholly removed from the influence of the spirit.'[3] What we should be looking for in such a service is not necessarily immediate physical change but a new orientation of body, mind and spirit.

Laying on of hands is preferably a shared act in which ordained and lay members of the church work together as an expression of the unity of the church in its faith and compassion. The invitation to come forward is probably best offered in the broadest terms to indicate that what we are concerned about is wholeness in its fullest sense of being completely reconciled to God. The invitation may then be addressed to those needing assurance of forgiveness, a new commitment to God, healing of body, mind and spirit, help in facing personal problems, their own or another's. It is often helpful if the people coming forward for healing are encouraged to say what their need is and whether the prayer is for themselves or for another. What we are doing is encouraging people to offer their situation to God, and a significant part of that situation may be their anxiety and concern for someone else.

This question of inviting those seeking healing to articulate their need and/or their concern for others, has caused some to speak about 'healing by proxy'. Just to put the matter in this way suggests a somewhat naive view of what is involved in such a service. At its heart the laying on of hands in a service for healing has the making explicit what is often implicit, namely our prayer and care for one another in the presence of God. The spiritual focus of this will always be the person who has come forward for ministry but it may also include others for whom that person has a serious concern. In this service, at the very least, the church is doing three things:

(i) encouraging people to offer up their situation to God and to share their concerns with a representative of that community of believers;

(ii) providing someone to listen to those concerns and to offer them to God in prayer;

(iii) offering the laying on of hands by two or three people as an effective sign of the church's care and compassion.

Objections to offering prayer for others than the one present suggest to me a failure to understand what we are about in such a service. It is also to fail to appreciate what is widely accepted in therapy today, namely the way in which one person may present in his or her own illness the dis-ease of another, or even a whole group of people, the family or neighbourhood. It also suggests an incomplete, because too individualistic, theology of salvation. Those who can say with Paul, 'as in Adam all die, so also in Christ shall all be made alive',[4] should not stumble at the organic, corporate models of thought that allow prayer to be offered for others, through others, at a service for healing.

Of course, not all services for healing will take this form. There will be many services where people simply come forward to the altar rail for a blessing, as they come forward for the elements of bread and wine at Communion. Each church will find its own way into these services. There is no way which will be absolutely right for all.

The question will sometimes be raised as to who may assist in such services. I have always suggested four criteria for those assisting in this way:
(i) they should have the confidence of the local church (i.e. they should not be self-appointed);
(ii) however simply, they should be able to articulate prayer on behalf of the church;
(iii) they should be able to express and embody the church's caring ministry;
(iv) there should be about them an openness to the Holy Spirit and a firm belief that God 'is able to do far more abundantly than all that we ask or think'.

The laying on of hands is a sign of the church's compassion and commitment to those who are sick or in any distress. It is saying, 'We are with you in prayer and we will continue to care.' It is not therefore some kind of holy hanky-panky but an important element in liturgy in which we declare God's love for all who are in need. It is often a means of making intelligible the idea of grace to many who have failed to grasp it before. The more we can make it a normal, rather than an extraordinary, aspect of our liturgy the better; but we should not be disturbed if from time to time God brings his own surprises. As John Richards has reminded us, if we are to embark upon the healing ministry, we must be prepared to face both 'the depth and the disturbance of Christ's healing work'.[5]

ANOINTING

Mark tells how Jesus sent out the twelve disciples to preach the message of the Kingdom: 'So they went out and preached that men should repent. And they cast out many demons, and anointed with oil many that were sick and healed them.'[6] In James 5:14 we have the counsel to the sick to 'call for the elders of the church, and let them pray over him, anointing him with oil in the name of the Lord . . .'.

The use of oil in anointing was no new thing. Both Jew and Gentile used the oil of anointing in religious rites of blessing or hallowing, and on the appointment of kings, prophets or high priests. Jesus was designated the 'Messiah' or 'Anointed One'. Anointing with oil was also used as a medical remedy. As early as the third century it is found amongst Church orders as a means of blessing. Raphael Frost has pointed out that during the Middle Ages a close association between sin and sickness led to anointing being seen as a supreme means of reconciliation with God. By the ninth century, the faithful were seeking anointing for the remission of their sins on their death-bed.[7] It was at this time that anointing with oil, which had been freely performed by lay people in the ministry of healing, became restricted to membership of the priesthood. It was from this priestly anointing that the Roman sacrament of Extreme Unction developed in the twelfth century.

The Council of Trent (1545–63) described Extreme Unction as a sacrament instituted by Christ and taught by St James, representing the grace of the Holy Spirit cleansing venial sin and comforting the infirm. The statement declared that the sick man 'sometimes obtains bodily health when it is expedient to his soul'. Anointing was to be given when the illness was grave but not necessarily beyond the hope of recovery. It might be repeated in certain circumstances, namely, if after recovery there was a relapse, or if a different disease was involved. So gradually Extreme Unction came to be regarded as the last sacrament which prepared the soul for heaven and the practice of anointing for physical healing largely died out in the Western Church.

For the Eastern Church, however, anointing with oil has always been an important ministry to the sick. It is seen as an encouragement to repentance and reconciliation from which physical healing might properly flow.

Within Protestantism, Luther and Calvin held that sickness can be a means of grace for deepening our knowledge of God and had reservations about the Church's healing ministry. Luther rightly held that the anointing in James 5 was for those who were sick, not those who were dying. Calvin went so far as to say that unction was 'neither a ceremony appointed by God nor has any promise'.[8] However, the Lutheran theologian Bengel and John Wesley both recognised anointing as a powerful means of healing in the Church.

More recently there has been a rediscovery of the practice of anointing with oil. Guide-lines for its use can be simply stated, though there may be variations in practice among the communions:

(i) it may take place in public or in private;

(ii) it may be within the context of a Communion service;

(iii) it will be closely linked with confession of sin and reassurance of pardon;

(iv) it will more usually be for those closely committed to the Church;

(v) it will be used more selectively than laying on of hands, though it can quite naturally take place alongside it;

(vi) it is usually with olive oil, often previously blessed by a bishop or church leader;

(vii) the thumb of the right hand is dipped into the oil and then placed on the forehead of the anointee with prayer, making the sign of the cross (some choose also to have the palms of the hands anointed in the same way).

Such a rubric should not be used to limit pastoral care and response. Pastoral sensitivity and understanding, arising from a knowledge of the particular situation, should determine when such a ministry is required and the form that it should take.

ON DEATH AND DYING

Some years ago I was told that a city councillor, one who had done much for the community, was in hospital suffering from terminal cancer. He was not a church-goer and had no local minister to visit him. I took the suggestion and went to see him week by week. One day I found him in some considerable distress and anger. Feeling very much at loss for words, I suggested that if he was angry with God he should tell God he was angry with him. My new friend gave me a withering look and then said: 'I'm not angry with God, I'm angry with people like you who know all the questions and none of the answers!' It was a cry of dereliction and I'm not sure that I was at that point ready to share it with him. I awarded myself no brownie points for that particular visit and promised to call again the following day. Later on I was more ready to share his grief and search for meaning.

If I had not known before, I knew at that time that few of us have any innate skill in prayer with, and pastoral care for, the dying. For various reasons we often appear less sensitive than we really are. In the desire to be helpful and in our anxiety to 'support' God, we tend to make statements instead of watching for signals and listening to spoken or unspoken cries. Sometimes we make the opposite mistake of remaining silent when perhaps we should speak with authority. Misunderstanding of others' roles and inter-professional anxieties only serve to aggravate the problem.

Improvement in communication in the face of death and the dying is probably one of the more urgent medical and pastoral requirements of our day. From the Hospice Movement, and more recently from treating AIDS sufferers, we have learned something about the need for appropriate terminal care. From organisations like Cruse and Compassionate Friends, we are learning how to enable the bereaved to face bereavement with support and friendship. There is still much to do if we are to cultivate a healthy attitude towards death and a truly supportive role towards the dying and the bereaved. Part of our difficulty is that whilst we are experts in our own experience, we cannot be sure that our experience can be used to help or describe another's. This is generally true when we are involved in a boundary experience like bereavement. It is particularly true when we are involved with those facing terminal illness because, presumably, we have never been in their position. If we are to be able to minister to those in that situation, it may be necessary for us to recognise that we are all in some sense terminal-care patients and thus able to see death as a blessed boundary.

One of the constant questions facing those who minister to the terminally ill is how much it is possible to share this realisation with them. There are some who, though they recognise the seriousness of their illness, refuse to acknowledge that they are about to die. Some will maintain this attitude of denial right up to the point of death. Others will hold to it for just a brief while; much depends upon their own temperament, upbringing and their relationships with others. Some will acknowledge this to their doctor or minister but refuse to do so to their next of kin. There are many more who, if they do not wish to be confronted directly with this fact, are willing to be led into a silent mutual acknowledgement of 'last things'. What they do not want is to be ignored or treated like children or non-persons when decisions are taken that affect their all too limited future. There comes a time when most will want to know the truth of their condition, or as much as they can bear at that time, in order that they may complete the essential pattern of their lives. Those at this stage welcome the opportunity to share some of their feelings and fears, especially those which would normally remain hidden. Then it is important that there should be someone on hand who will really listen, rather than offer smooth words from a safe distance.

In every situation it is important that the dying should be allowed to retain as long as possible their personal dignity, and to the end, their sense of self-worth and value in the sight of God. An essential part of this self-worth is the sense of hope, the recognition that all is not lost, that there are still things to be done, relationships to be enjoyed, precious experiences to be shared. It would be unrealistic to expect the terminal state to be only a felicitous one, however. Along with moments of hope and reconsideration of priorities there will also be times of helplessness and weakness. Then it is important that there should be someone, not some great bringer of light, but one who can be trusted to go with them through the darkness and hold them until they see the light again. If there is one demand that every dying person should be able to make it is that they should know that in that difficult journey into the unknown they will not be abandoned. For it is not death itself so much as the process of dying that brings most fear.

The important ministry at this time is, as far as possible, to help people overcome this fear of dying and to enable them to know that there is love and power available whatever life or death can bring. Usually a simple prayer, following a word of promise from the Bible, as in Psalm 23 or Romans 8:38–9, is of greater value than any offering of our own tenuous and tight-lipped hope. It is one of the surprises of divine grace that it is often those who have reached this boundary and looked over who are able to lead us and lift us as they share their own inner peace and confidence that nothing will be lost and all will be well.

Blessed be the God and Father of our Lord Jesus Christ, the Father of mercies and God of all comfort, who comforts us in all our affliction, so that we may be able to comfort those who are in any affliction, with the comfort with which we ourselves are comforted by God.[9]

Towards a Working Theology

Some approach theology as an academic discipline, a corpus of knowledge, others as a way of interpreting and responding to events, experiences and relationships in the light of our faith in God. It is in this latter sense that I am using it here. In these terms, anyone who suggests that he or she can provide 'the theology' of anything is most likely to be either a rogue or a charlatan, or probably both, and should be regarded with due suspicion. It may be possible to discuss the theology which lies behind the work of a particular 'healer', say Brother Mandus, Harry Edwards or John Wimber. Equally it may be possible to discuss the theology which lay behind healing in the Old Testament or the New Testament, or even that which lies behind our National Health Service today. That is probably as far as we can go in any direct and definitive way.

At the same time it is important, if that which can be a 'many splendour'd thing' is not to become a minefield, that there should be some exploration into the theological issues which underlie the churches' healing ministry.

Fundamental to an understanding of Christian healing is the character of God, the nature of the human predicament and the saving activity of God in Jesus Christ. In the chapter on the biblical tradition it was affirmed that one of the characteristics of God's creation is that it is essentially good. God loves that which he has made and longs for its perfection. He loves without distinction and without limit. As Hans Küng has said, 'The will of God is the well-being of man'. The Bible speaks of human disobedience bringing a fall from grace, whereby disorder was brought to God's world. The story of Adam's fall provides a telling reminder of that which contemporary society is always trying to avoid, namely a recognition of the sheer fallibility and fragility of the human condition.

We cannot lightly slough off the effects of our fallen condition, but neither should we underestimate the power and purpose of God to restore harmony to his creation. The Old Testament points forward to the deliverance that God will bring in the coming of the Messiah, who will

> preach good news to the poor,
> . . . proclaim release to the captives
> and recovering of sight to the blind,
> . . . set at liberty those who are oppressed,
> . . . proclaim the acceptable year of the Lord.[1]

WHAT DOES IT MEAN TO BE HUMAN AND TO BE HEALTHY?

The New Testament generally answers the question 'What is man?' by pointing to Christ. Behold the man, the great exemplar of what it means to be human, but also the Liberator, the one through whom the forces of evil are dethroned and by whom we are to be set free to have life in all its fulness.

We are not to take lightly this crucial encounter in which cosmic powers are mightily engaged. P. T. Forsyth has written:

The grand human strike against God would ruin both the workers and the Master, did He not, in His love's tremendous resource, find means over their heads to save both His cause and theirs out of the wreck. Human misery is too great for the human power of pity. No heart but that of holy God is equal to inviting into it all that labour and are heavy laden, to pitying on an adequate scale the awful tragedy of man or measuring man's suffering with that informed sympathy which is the condition of healing it.[2]

To participate in the Church's ministry of healing is to bear witness that we are sharing in a crucial encounter in which alien powers are similarly involved. This does not mean that we are to see demons behind every bush or tree. It is necessary to recognise, however, that the battle in which we are engaged does involve good and evil, in many and various forms. Our comfort lies in the knowledge that *the* crucial encounter took place on Calvary and we are engaged in what might be termed the 'mopping up' operations.

In 1964 the Tübingen Consultation on *The Healing Church* reported: 'The specific character of the Christian understanding of health and healing arises from its place in the whole Christian belief about God's plan of salvation for mankind.'[3] In the specifically Christian part of the story, this begins with the incarnation, the breaking into human history of God in human form. It continues in the ministry of Jesus in which we see the powers of the Kingdom of God becoming engaged with, and then overcoming, the powers of evil. Here we see that health in these terms is more than just the attainment of a balance in the human equilibrium. It is not a static but a dynamic concept, involving a continuing encounter with the problems of human guilt, suffering and death.

I refer to that Tübingen Consultation again:

Health, in the Christian understanding, is a continuous and victorious encounter with the powers that deny the existence and goodness of God. It is a participation in an invasion of the realm of evil, in which the final victory lies beyond death, but the power of that victory is known now in the life-giving Spirit. It is the kind of life which has overcome death and the anxiety which is the shadow of death. Whether in the desperate squalor of over-populated and undeveloped areas, or in the spiritual wasteland of affluent societies, it is a sign of God's victory and a summons to his service.[4]

In the light of this, it is clear that health, in its fullest sense, is more than just efficient functioning or physical well-being. It involves both soul and body and an essential harmony between the two – a harmony that derives from the power of the soul to cope with the varying conditions of the body.

The Christian will also ask whether a single-minded pursuit

of health for its own sake is actually a symptom of deficient health, and even perhaps another kind of idolatry. The question must always be about health or fitness for what? Health is not a final end; it is a means of glorifying God and being able to fulfil his purpose. So we should desire it and work for it, as it provides the capacity, the vitality and the freedom to exercise the physical, social and spiritual functions which are part of our responsibility as children of God.

The Christian understanding of health and healing is developed by a recognition of its place in the life and ministry of Jesus. His healing ministry bore eloquent testimony not just to his compassion but even more to who and what he was. So in the fourth Gospel, we find the man who was blind from birth responding at first to those who asked who it was who had healed him by saying: 'He is a prophet.'[5] Later, when they continued to press him, he responded angrily, 'If this man were not from God, he could do nothing.' In all that he said and did, Jesus made plain that the source and centre of that saying and doing was God the Father, the prime mover in all his life and ministry. Shortly before the promise of the Comforter, Jesus said to the disciples: 'The words that I say to you I do not speak on my own authority; but the Father who dwells in me does his works.'[6] It was this relationship with God, so intimate that Jesus could speak of being in the Father and the Father in him, that provided the authority and the power for his healing work. For the Christian, true humanity and true health consists in this kind of intimate, obedient and dependent relationship with the Father, through Jesus his Son. In this sense, of course, we all fall lamentably short.

In a splendid piece of symbolism, Donald Baillie imagines God calling his human children to form a great circle 'for the playing of his game'. They are to stand with hands linked lovingly together, facing towards the light in the centre, which is God, and seeing our fellows all round the circle in the light of that central love, which shines on them and gives beauty to them. Instead of that, Baillie suggests, 'we have each one turned our backs upon God and upon the circle of our fellows, and faced the other way, so that we can see neither the Light at the centre nor the faces on the circumference.'[7]

There is much in the Bible to suggest that health can be defined in terms of right relationships:
(i) a relationship with God, expressed in our obedience to his will and a response to him in love and worship;
(ii) a relationship to our whole selves, accepting every part of our being as given by God and therefore to be treated with respect and love;
(iii) a relationship to our neighbour, expressed in love and service;
(iv) a relationship to our environment, expressed in concern and stewardship.

Throughout the Bible we see the mystery of our humanity being discovered in an understanding of the whole: the whole universe, the whole community, the whole person, the whole experience of life in its totality. This involves a continuity with all that has gone before, with what is yet to be and with all around us at the present.

HEALING AND SALVATION

The words healing and salvation both point to ways in which God acts towards his people. Christian theology has sought to maintain the relationship between the two and has usually done this by making healing subordinate to salvation. As we are becoming increasingly aware they have much in common. John Wycliffe and William Tyndale, whose translations of the Bible precede that of the Authorised Version, both use the word *heelthe* regularly to translate the Vulgate *salus*, i.e. salvation. So in Luke 1:69,71,77 Wycliffe has:

> And he hath rerid to us an horn of heelthe in the hous of David, his child . . . Helthe fro oure enemyes, and fro the hoond of alle men that hatiden us . . . To gyve scyence of helthe to his puple, in to remyssioun of her [=their] synnes. ['knowledge of salvation' RSV]

In Luke 19:9ff:

For to dai heelthe is maad to this hous, for that he [Zac-
chaeus] is Abraham's sone; for mannus sone cam to seke,
and to make saaf that thing that perischide. ['Today salvation
has come to this house' RSV]

He(e)lthe is used for *salus* each time, whether it refers to safety
from enemies or forgiveness of sins. For the adjective *salvus*,
Wycliffe uses *saaf*, so in Mark 5:34:

Dougter, thi feith hath maad thee saaf; go in pees, and be
thou hool of thi sijknesse.

Hool is, of course, the corresponding adjective to the noun
heelthe. What we may assume from this is that in Wycliffe's
day (fourteenth century), *heelthe* had a broader meaning than
today and could be used to translate the equally broad Vulgate
word *salus*, covering physical safety and religious salvation. On
the other hand when an adjective was required for *salvus*,
covering 'whole' of body or 'saved' of soul, the choice was for
saaf.[8]

The root meaning of the Old Testament word for salvation
is spaciousness, enlargement. The word the New Testament
uses for salvation or deliverance, in the Greek, is *soteria*. The
word has both a general and a particular meaning. In general,
it means release from difficulty, danger, loss or crippling cir-
cumstance. In particular, it means deliverance from sin and its
consequences, and the coming to peace and reconciliation with
God.

Salvation, like healing, has both an individual and a corporate reference. Whilst suffering is not necessarily the consequence of individual sin, sin may be the cause of suffering
both for the individual and also for others. I remember as a
schoolboy, on an exchange visit to Germany, sitting in the
Olympic Stadium when Adolf Hitler gave a stirring address to
the many thousands gathered there. It was just two years before
the outbreak of war with Germany. At that time Hitler was at
the height of his powers but the triumphal atmosphere of that
occasion gave little indication of the horrendous violence that
was shortly to break out upon Europe and beyond.

It was the sin of pride, riding on the injustices of the Versailles Treaty, that eventually brought such a wave of destructiveness and horror upon the whole world. Had there been no Hitler, it is possible that we should not have had to endure the horrors of Belsen, the ruin of great cities and the loss of many precious lives. In this sense there is always the possibility of a causal relationship between sin and sickness. The Bible warns us not to underestimate the way that the whole body can suffer because of the sin of one, and also of the collective sickness that follows upon corporate sin. This comes upon us because of our falling away from our origin in God, individually and collectively, and leads to a letting loose of destructiveness seen in a powerful form on Calvary but seen also in different ways throughout the whole of human life.

So there is a kind of sickness, a form of alienation which belongs to our condition but from which God purposes to deliver us through the gift of his Son and the working of the Holy Spirit. Paul cried:

> We know that the whole creation has been groaning in travail together until now; and not only the creation, but we ourselves, who have the first fruits of the Spirit, groan inwardly as we wait for adoption as sons, the redemption of our bodies. For in this hope we were saved.[9]

Here healing, redemption, salvation are seen against their true background, not of the individual alone but of the creation as a whole. Healing belongs to the infrastructure, not just to human beings but also the birds of the air and the stones of the earth. The promise continues with the triumphant assurance:

> neither death, nor life, nor angels, nor principalities, nor things present, nor things to come, nor powers, nor height, nor depth, nor anything else in all creation, will be able to separate us from the love of God in Christ Jesus our Lord.[10]

To accept this is to accept the healing par excellence: the unity, the wholeness, of the Creator with his creation. This is salvation – not something that comes through the strenuous pursuit of evolutionary development, nor, as some would seek to assure us, a continual increase in the gross national product. It is the response of faith and love to the initiative by God that all relationships might be restored: the relationship between the created and the Creator, between human beings and their environment, between individuals and their community, between the various elements in human personality.

Salvation, then, is seen as God's action towards his people in the overcoming of alienation by atonement and is more fittingly predicated of the community than of the individual. The Old Testament knows very little of individual salvation. The people of Israel had a well-developed community structure and lived under a group covenant with God. Indeed it is God, who, through his covenant with Israel, provides the locus of community. When one member suffers, the community suffers with him; when one member sins, the whole community is involved. This does not mean that the individual is relieved of personal responsibility. The eighth-century BC prophets, Amos, Hosea and Micah, call passionately for social justice, but it is all under a general injunction to Israel as a people. The true discovery of the individual comes later in the nation's history. As personal responsibility is seen against the background of community responsibility, so salvation is seen not so much as a gift to the individual as to the community. The individual participates in this gift in so far as he or she belongs to the people of God. In those days they really would not have known what to make of someone who said that there is no such thing as society!

It is not surprising, then, that the Hebrew people saw the salvation of the community as being accomplished by the coming of a Messiah, the one in whom the essential wholeness of the community might be restored and its unity be made manifest.

Paul was being true to this tradition when, in his letter to the Colossians, he saw Christ as the one who came to restore wholeness to the whole creation: 'For in him [Christ] all the fullness of God was pleased to dwell, and through him to reconcile to himself all things, whether on earth or in heaven, making peace by the blood of his cross.'[11] It is true that the

apostle went on to speak about individuals 'who were once
estranged and hostile in mind, doing evil deeds' and have now
been reconciled by Christ, in order that they might be presented
holy and blameless before him. The redemption that Paul is
referring to is a redemption of body and soul within the individual and of individuals within their society and their world.
Although salvation may begin for me with me, it is for all
people, and for all people not in isolation but in community.
It is a total redemption to which God calls us in Jesus Christ.
The object of redemption is no less than that of the whole
cosmos. Christ, who is the centre and substance of the divine
event, is Lord of the universe, the image of the incarnate God.

From now on, to be saved, to be whole, means to stand in
a mature and harmonious relationship with the whole creation
and with God himself, after the pattern of Jesus Christ. Emphasis is here being placed upon the corporate nature of salvation
because so many of the distortions that arise within the Christian healing ministry spring from an excessive individualism in
which the corporate nature of our being has been neglected.
Implicit in the New Testament teaching about salvation is the
assumption that our sickness cannot be divorced from our predicament as a whole. Sickness is only one sign of our estrange-
ment from God and from those structures through which we
discover relationships with our neighbour and our environment.
By the same token, healing of the individual is just one way in
which God's redemptive power is bestowed.

When Mr Shevardnadze, the Soviet Foreign Minister, speaking in the United Nations, pleads for steps to be taken to
protect the world and its environment, he is adding weight to
the statement of the Dutch theologian, Edward Schillebeeckx,
who has suggested that salvation, once of interest only to
religious people, has now become 'the great stimulus throughout our contemporary human existence, the driving force of all
human history'. So now it is no longer only theologians and
churchmen who are striving for salvation but also politicians,
statesmen and environmentalists.

Sometimes, it seems, the Church might learn from such
people particularly if our view of salvation has become too
individualistic or negative. I remember hearing a deaconess

speaking on the Sunday morning radio programme at five to eight. She was attempting to answer the question about what the Church was doing: what good things she was seeing in her parish. She spoke of a young man who swears less now that he has been converted and a young girl who formerly slept around who is now a reformed character. The deaconness rightly saw this as being a good thing, as indeed it is. The difficulty arises in the choice of good things that were described and the model of salvation that was being suggested. Sometimes we need to be reminded that Christianity is not principally about sin but about forgiveness: the love of God in Jesus by which we are able to find hope, deliverance and renewal. The idea of the exorcising of evil, as a principal Christian strategy, is an extremely seductive one. For one thing it enables us to localise sin within the individual and to see it, not as a relational disorder within the person and between that person and his/her environment, but as something discrete and objective for which we can offer deliverance.

Some years ago I was asked by a local GP, a woman I had worked with on previous occasions, to give pastoral help to a disturbed young woman who was going through a marriage break-up and the possibility of losing custody of two of her children. When I learned that part of her disturbance derived from a sexual trauma she had experienced as a young girl, I immediately suggested that my woman colleague might take her on. 'Oh no,' said the doctor, 'it must be a man; someone highly responsible and totally unseducible!' 'Thank you very much!' I replied. I saw this young woman for one hour a week, every week, for two years until the home and family situation had been stabilised and she was more competent to cope with her problems. When I mentioned this person and her problems to a colleague who was at that time heavily into exorcism, he replied almost dismissively, 'Oh, you should have given her exorcism. You could have saved yourself all that time!'

The dominant concept of healing (saving) as the eradication of disease (sin) is seductive also in that it sets apart those who are sick from those who are the healers, the deliverers. This may be reassuring and prestige-enhancing for the healers without really bringing a corresponding benefit to the sufferers. It may also be dangerous, if it leads us to suppose that by exorcising evil we can quickly and easily provide the solution to a problem without having to give thought to the complexities underlying it, and our responsibility to tackle the possible causes.

In Christian terms we need a soteriology that goes beyond the removal of evil and gives major emphasis to a strengthening of the good and a profound re-ordering of life. Jesus did not offer Zacchaeus an exorcism. He offered him a new way of life that involved a new standing before God and a new relationship with those whom he had wronged.[12] In this way goodness becomes more real than badness. God becomes more real than the devil. In medical terms we have seen how emphasis upon defects leads to a pathology that is more real than health. This can lead to precious resources being concentrated upon dramatic interventionist kinds of treatment rather than upon disease management, continuing care, positive preventative practices and life-style changes. Of course we rejoice in the development of surgery and are profoundly grateful for the marvels accomplished by it. It is, however, only a part of the total medical scene. We have to become increasingly conscious of the danger of that lack of balance which enables people to suggest that what we have in Britain today is not a National Health Service but a National Sickness Service. Perhaps we should be giving more attention to developing the fulness of human potential, to strengthening strengths, to developing what is known in the army as morale, to initiating and encouraging new ways of being healthy. This might be more creative, and in the long run less expensive, than pursuing a medical model that seems to concentrate on the removal of defects.

Pauline Webb recalls the compulsive gambler describing the help he had received through Gamblers Anonymous, which had enabled him to put together the broken wreck of his life, to find a new job, to be reconciled to his wife, to pay back his debts, to reform his habits. Summing it all up, he said: 'I've been saved – no, I'm not using that word in a religious sense. I mean really saved.' For him the religious word had lost its meaning. But the experience was real. He had found salvation in the restoration of his whole life in its social context. He was

referring to the way in which as a person he was now functioning in a better, more complete, more whole way.

If in the act of salvation God accepts us for what we are, by
that same act he also confirms us in what we ought to be. So
there is a continuing obligation to ask ourselves: saved for
what? just as we were compelled to ask: health for what? Two
considerations come immediately to mind.

Salvation involves a proper stewardship of our resources.
This means that we have to consider very carefully how we
relate to, and use, the world's natural resources, how we treat
the environment. In the political sense it means a critical
approach to the earthly power-systems and maintenance of 'a
bias to the poor'. It also means careful concern for the way we
deal with urban priority areas, health care, education and other
important national resources. In the personal sense it means
examination of our giving and spending with the recognition
that the giving of ourselves and our gifts to God and his Kingdom is not without significant consequences. In the same way
the withholding of ourselves and our gifts from God is not
without equally significant consequences. Unless we are prepared to take this seriously we are in grave danger of living in
one kingdom at one point of our lives and in another kingdom
at another. That way lies disharmony and disintegration and is
not a good prescription for healthy living.

Salvation for the Christian also means to be enlisted in
Christ's service. It is to be understood that this can mean afflic-
tions as well as conquests. As many Christians in Latin America
and similar situations have discovered, preaching good news,
proclaiming release to the captives and setting at liberty those
who are oppressed, is to be enlisted in Christ's continuing
warfare in which there are wounds as well as honours and in
which we may, as Paul put it, be 'consigned to our death every
day, for the sake of Jesus'. In the glorious paradox of the
gospel this is one of the ways in which wounds are turned into
honours 'so that in our mortal flesh the life of Jesus, too, may
be openly shown'.[13]

In his prayer for the Thessalonians, Paul says: 'May the God
of peace himself sanctify you wholly; and may your spirit and
soul and body be kept sound and blameless at the coming of

our Lord Jesus Christ.'[14] This suggests that salvation has both a present and a future reference. We may sample it, delight in it in the present and yet recognise that this is but a foretaste of something yet to be. We cannot really know salvation in all its fulness until we are brought to that more spacious, more liberating day 'at the coming of our Lord Jesus Christ'.

HEALING AND CURING

Writing recently in one of our Renewal magazines, a minister protested in strong terms at 'the way in which the concept of healing has been broadened until it is more or less all-embracing'.[15] He went on to affirm with some justification that 'in the New Testament in the vast majority of instances healing means curing someone's physical ailment'. For this minister the 'healing of relationships', 'the healing of the environment' and the 'healing which is death' are simply diversions which detract from the responsibility of addressing ourselves to the major task of preaching the good news of the Kingdom and giving evidence that we accept the commission: 'Heal the sick, raise the dead, cleanse those who have leprosy, drive out demons'.[16]

It is difficult not to have great sympathy with the writer, especially as he goes on to relate how his teen-age son lay in intensive care after a road accident and subsequently died, although he and his wife had prayed for life for him.

Those of us who have been involved in the healing ministry know all too well the danger of making 'healing' such an umbrella word that eventually it loses all meaning. I take comfort, however, that this is no new phenomenon. I have recently been drawing together a list of some of the instances in which our hymn-writers use the word 'healing' in this broad, all-embracing way, and often as a substitute for 'salvation':

William Cowper rejoices, 'It is the Lord who rises with healing in His wings'. (Sometimes a light surprises)
Somerset Corry Lowry prays that God will 'Heal our wrongs, and help our need'. (Son of God, eternal Saviour)

Joachin Neander bids us, 'praise Him, for He is thy health
and salvation'. (Praise to the Lord, the Almighty)
Dorothy Angus speaks of humankind coming 'To the manger
humbly kneeling', and then continues, 'Still they come for
help and healing'. (Once there came to earth)
Fred Kaan, more recently, bids us pray, 'For the healing of
the nations'.

We are perhaps fortunate in this country in that we have the
words 'to heal' and 'to cure'. The French have only one word,
guérir, which means either to heal or to cure. This makes it
difficult in any Anglo-French exchange of medical people. They
are then required to speak of 'curing a disease' or 'healing the
person'. Perhaps this is no bad thing in that it makes for clarity
of discourse. In English, when using a purely physical model
of health, the two words can be used almost synonymously.
For those who do not accept a purely physical model, it is
important that a proper distinction should be made. Cure normally implies 'the complete removal of a disease agency from
the body, along with its accompanying symptoms and physical
signs'. Healing 'refers to that progress to wholeness of body,
mind and spirit which is never completely realised in this life'.[17]
It is a much broader concept than cure and indicates wider
possibilities. So one may know cure without true healing and
healing without being cured.

The story of the ten lepers[18] is often cited as an instance of
the former. All ten were cured of their leprosy but only one
returned to give thanks. This seemed to indicate to Jesus a
certain deformity of character which called in question the
quality and extent of the healing. In the same way we have
seen people go into hospital and receive skilled surgery and
much tender loving care, but on their discharge they give no
evidence that they have learned from their experience or grown
as human beings. They may have been cured but have they
been healed? A surgeon, with a sense of humour, and a Christian conviction apparent to his patients, told of one of his
patients who had to undergo a complicated operation about
the issue of which the surgeon himself was doubtful. Before
the operation the patient was afraid, but committed himself to

the surgeon and the surgeon's trust in God. When informed that the operation had been successful, he devoutly cried 'Thank God'. When a month later he was told that he had made excellent progress, he again thanked God, but more faintly. But when, a considerable while after, he was asked about his operation by an acquaintance, he said he had come through it, adding proudly, 'But then I have a very strong constitution!'[19] One wonders just how much he had learned from his illness.

On the other hand, we have all known people whose response to suffering has been of such a kind that they give daily evidence of a healing which is more wonderful than physical cure. A very dear friend of mine, Elizabeth Twistington Higgins, is one of those who have wrestled with physical infirmity for years, have found no quick or easy answer to their problems but have achieved an enviable poise and power.

Elizabeth was stricken with poliomyelitis at the age of thirty and became paralysed from chest to foot. Once a ballet dancer with a professional company in London, she was reduced to living in an iron-lung. For many years she fought frustration and bitterness, knowing that bitterness has no part in the healing process. She also fought her disability. Eventually she was able to come out of the iron-lung during the daytime, until recently returning to hospital every evening. During these past thirty years, from her wheelchair, and with the aid of some remarkable technology and the help of many friends, she has attained to a life of astonishing creativity and usefulness. She has taught ballet and seen her girls dance in village halls and stately cathedrals. She has painted pictures, written books, appeared on television and done lots of things which many able-bodied people have not been able to do.

Elizabeth has not been cured, but she demonstrates in a remarkable manner that wholeness is not about physical perfection, but more about how we respond to the gifts which God has given to us and the challenges which life presents to us. It is about how we accept joy and sorrow, how we cope with pain and suffering, or, as she might say, how we share together in the dance of life. Often I have come away, after visiting her, challenged and rebuked, knowing that she is more whole than I am.

Yet perhaps that minister, whose protest I began with, has a point. Perhaps the Church does need to recover its nerve where Christian healing is concerned. In many ways it is true that our lack of power derives not from any withdrawal of God's gifts to the Church but from the fact that we have failed to make them our own. Morton T. Kelsey suggests:

The Church speaks of miracles like a public exhibition once staged, but overlooks the desire of God to be sought and his ability to step into the immediate physical world specifically, creatively with healing. The almost unbelievable power of God to love, to care for the created world has been pushed further and further out of the picture.[20]

One of the charges that Alexander Solzhenitsyn, the Soviet dissident, laid against western society was that we had pushed God further and further out of the picture so that he no longer had any relevance for us and we had no expectations of him. Whatever the reason for our reluctance to claim God's healing power, it does seem that we have become too faint-hearted in our petitionary approach to God and this is plainly against the grain of Jesus' teaching.

Ask, and it will be given you; seek, and you will find; knock, and it will be opened to you.[21]
If you then, who are evil, know how to give good gifts to your children, how much more will your Father who is in heaven give good things to those who ask him![22]

The story is told of a Lancashire woman who was greatly troubled about the huge coal tip that over the years had grown right outside her back door, taking away the light from her house during the winter and blocking her view of the surrounding countryside during the summer. One day she approached her minister to ask: 'Do you think that if I prayed for this to be removed, the good Lord would move it?' The minister considered for a time and then replied: 'Well, the Bible does say something about if we have faith and doubt not, then we can say to a mountain, "be removed and cast into the sea" and it shall be done. I should try it.' The minister saw his parishioner a week later and asked how she had got on. 'Well,' said the woman, 'I prayed that it should be removed but it's still there, as I expected it would be!'

Too often, it seems, our attitude to prayer is of this negative, cautious and unexpectant nature. If the Church owes anything to the Charismatic Movement, it is surely the emphasis upon the need for Christians to be more open to God, more expectant in faith and hope. Jesus taught that faith is a powerful weapon in the armoury which God has provided for our encounter with evil, from whatever source it may come. Too often, probably fearing a failure in response, we have underplayed the possibilities of faith and hope, forgetting that God is on the side of health and healing and this does mean physical as well as spiritual healing.

I think of a little girl of five who had cancer of the kidney, which spread to the lungs. She had the benefit of skilled surgery and all the resources of a wonderful hospital and a caring staff. She had the powerful support and love of her family and friends and a local church. But above all she had the unshakeable faith of her mother that she would be restored to health. Some, from the very best of motives, expressed anxiety about this. 'We mustn't allow her to build her hopes too high. Just think of the effect it will have if . . .' The word death was not so much mentioned as implied. In fact, after further surgery to remove nodules on both lungs, Samantha has been discharged from hospital with every hope of a full recovery. Her hair has grown again and she is dancing around as lively and full of mischief as any other six-year-old.

At this point it is perhaps not inappropriate to remind ourselves that one of the misconceptions about the Church's healing ministry is that an unexplained, in some terms 'supernatural', healing is more wonderful than one which can be understood. I would not for one moment deny the possibility of supernatural healing. On the basis that what is affirmed is more important than what is denied, I would want to affirm the importance of healing on the basis of creation and redemption. That means that I see God present in 'natural' as well as 'supernatural' means. The tendency of many of the new religious movements to see God at work only in the supernatural and to write off as of lesser importance what is sometimes described as 'secular' activity, I see as diminishing the biblical doctrine of God as a God of creation and redemption. To diminish the importance in the divine scheme of things of the skill of doctors or the care of nurses, even by implication, is to run into grave danger of denying the God who is immanent in his creation.

Samantha's healing was effected by a great many factors in which the love of God was reflected and by which his purposes were fulfilled: the skill of the doctors, the care of the nurses, the overarching provision of a great modern hospital, the prayers of the Church (which included specific pastoral care by hospital chaplains and local ministers) and the love and faith of those parents. For all this we can and should give glory to God.

It should be clear from all that has gone before that absolutely fundamental to our approach to the healing ministry of the Church will be our understanding of the nature of God. This then must be our next concern.

10

The God Who Heals

When seeking for an understanding of God in the pages of the Bible, it is probably wise to take a broad view, remembering that it encompasses something like one thousand years of teaching and writing. The character of God presented here is many faceted, gradually developing and essentially panoramic in view.

We shall be looking later at the graphic account of God's intervention in Eden, when we consider the question of the Fall. At this stage it is worth pausing at the haunting sentence in which the writer describes the plight of Adam and Eve, after taking the forbidden fruit: 'And they heard the sound of the Lord God walking in the garden in the cool of the day, and the man and his wife hid themselves from the presence of the Lord God among the trees of the garden.'[1] The picture reminds me of the much loved labrador dog we had in our family, who, having stolen food in the kitchen and being reprimanded, would slope off into his box, eyes down and ears and tail sagging. He, noble animal that he was, recognised that his function was to keep us company and guard the family's interests, and he had let us down. His penitence was usually short-lived and soon he would be bouncing around with the children, as if the incident had never happened. Good relationships, however, were important to him. It was just sad that labradors seem to be born with an infinite capacity for food, as well as for human company and love. How many of us suffer periodically, if not permanently, from a similar sense of guilt and shame? The sickness we present is often the result of this guilt, arising from a broken relationship and a longing for reconciliation. Forgiveness, though not impossible, seems difficult to come by.

How much more difficult it must have been in the far-off days of Eden. The picture there is not of a mildly irritated God, who puts on a show of anger, almost for form's sake, but that of a righteous, implacable God, who will tolerate no disobedience or rivalry, and says to Adam:

> In the sweat of your face
> you shall eat bread
> till you return to the ground,
> for out of it you were taken;
> you are dust,
> and to dust you shall return.[2]

Adam was driven out of Eden 'to till the ground from which he was taken'.

As we move on through the Old Testament, we find the people of Israel in slavery in Egypt. The picture now is of a God who longs for his people's return and is prepared to take their side against Pharaoh. Moses is God's agent to bring them from slavery to freedom. It is, however, a long and bitter struggle, with Pharaoh calling upon the Israelites to make bricks without straw and the Lord subjecting the Egyptians to innumerable hurts, to much disease and death before the Israelites were delivered from bondage.

Then followed that long and circuitous journey to the promised land, with all the problems of change involved in a nomadic people settling to life in a strange community and amongst foreign peoples. The picture now is of a God of mercy and forgiveness, but one with whom it is better to take no liberties. There is a clear touch of 'be sure your sins will find you out'. This is essentially a God of the Ten Commandments, whose law is inscribed on tables of stone. Though he loves his people, he will not hesitate to visit the iniquity of the fathers upon the children and the children's children.

By the eighth century BC we are given new insight into the character of the God of Israel. Hosea is as intense and as inflexible as Amos in his moral indignation against human wickedness. There is, however, a new and tender note in his teaching. Out of his own experience of unfaltering love for an

unfaithful wife, Hosea came to see something of the love and
sorrow that lives in the heart of God. There is in his teaching
the first glimpse of a new revelation, of a tender God, one who
yearns over his wayward people and is ready to offer forgiveness and bring healing. So Hosea writes:

> When Israel was a child, I loved him,
> and out of Egypt I called my son.
> The more I called them,
> the more they went from me; . . .

> Yet it was I who taught Ephraim [Israel] to walk,
> I took them up in my arms;
> but they did not know that I healed them . . .

> How can I give you up, O Ephraim! . . .
> My heart recoils within me,
> my compassion grows warm and tender.
> I will not execute my fierce anger,
> I will not again destroy Ephraim;
> for I am God and not man,
> the Holy One in your midst,
> and I will not come to destroy.[3]

Here we see the beginnings of the idea of healing as the
granting and acceptance of forgiveness. We are also led gently
to a view of the God who is both near and far. God is the Holy
One in the midst, a beguiling introduction to the wonder of
the incarnation.

GOD AS REDEEMER AND SOVEREIGN LORD

It is Karl Barth who, in our day, has reminded us that God's
creative sovereignty is conveyed in his communication. It is
through Jesus Christ, his breaking into time and space, his life,
death and resurrection, that God confirms the story of his
covenant with Israel and initiates a new covenant with the New
Israel:

In many and various ways God spoke of old to our fathers by the prophets; but in these last days he has spoken to us by a Son, whom he appointed the heir of all things, through whom also he created the world. He reflects the glory of God and bears the very stamp of his nature, upholding the universe by his word of power.[4]

According to this tradition, the whole universe coheres through Christ and is to be the expression of his glory. The new covenant in Christ is one which embraces the whole world of human experience. The glory is to be seen in a harmonious partnership between heaven and earth, between God and his people, which suggests that God is reaching out to us with his energising power, very much as we see in the Michelangelo fresco of the creation in the Sistine Chapel.

Here we see that God, the Creator of the universe and Father of our Lord Jesus Christ, is for us; he wills our good and has articulated that will in the giving of his Son. That will for us is not without its moral and ethical implications. We are to be the children of God and it is in the searching for, and doing of, that will that we discover his nature and purpose. It is also in this way that we discover our own true health and healing.

The Bible, however, recognises with stark reality the ambivalent and paradoxical nature of our response to God's goodness. Knowledge of the good, the ideal of 'health', does not lead automatically to its accomplishment. It seems there is a certain flaw or fault deeply ingrained in the human condition. Made in the image and likeness of God, we simply do not reflect that image. In the words of the Prayer Book, 'there is no health in us'. This is simply and yet profoundly stated in Paul's great confession: 'For I do not do the good I want, but the evil that I do not want is what I do. Now if I do what I do not want, it is no longer I that do it, but sin which dwells within me.'[5] On this James Denney cogently comments: 'That might be antinomian, or manichean, as well as evangelical. A true saint may say it in a passion, but a sinner had better not make it a principle.'[6] Saint or sinner, we all know the truth to which Paul was referring and we recognise that it points to something elemental in our make-up. It is an element which is dramatically suggested in the story of the Fall – a graphic biblical description of our dilemma, going back to that first man and woman in the Garden of Eden, who sought independence of God and ate of the fruit of the tree of knowledge of good and evil. The consequences of this are felt in various ways but not least in a power of disorder which threatens creation on the one hand and yet on the other is an instrument of God's righteous judgement. This power is opposed to God's will as Creator and Father, and, as Karl Barth put it, 'has existence and power only under his mighty No'.[7]

Professor James Stewart warns us against neglecting or underestimating this fundamental element in biblical theology. He suggests that, in our desire for psychological interpretation of Romans 7, in terms of a divided self, we have lost something vital. In particular we have lost the sense of a cosmic battle and so the emphasis which is really at issue in the age-long tragic dilemma.

> What in fact is always at stake in every moment of temptation, is not a higher self or a lower self, personal integrity or dishonour – that is the least of it: what is at stake is the strengthening or (please God) the weakening of the spirit forces of evil that are out to destroy the kingdom of Christ.[8]

This, Stewart maintains, is the insight which we have too often lost in our theological reconstructions. So we have also lost 'Paul fighting with wild beasts at Ephesus, and Luther flinging his ink-pot at the devil'. But more seriously still, the loss is seen in a diminishing of the doctrine of the atonement.

Certainly the New Testament does seem to take more seriously than we do today the demonic element in human life. Paul, always aware of the victory of Calvary, recognised that the powers of evil, even though subject to God's 'mighty No', were still around and still oppressively bearing down. He recognised that the only hope was to be 'in Christ', to be so completely identified with him in his life, death and resurrection that the spirits of darkness could be put to flight. Whilst being careful not to give undue place to the demonic, we might recognise that there is some evidence to suggest that a purely revelatory concept of the atonement, in terms of God's constraining love, is not enough. We must not lose sight of the fierceness of the conflict with the principalities and powers, in which Christ was engaged on Calvary, or in which we are, or should be, engaged today. There may be some differences amongst us as to the nature of the principalities and powers and the hierarchy of their devilishness; there should be no quarrel about the fact of the conflict.

James Stewart is careful to suggest that if there is a weakness in Bishop Aulen's *Christus Victor* view of the atonement, it is that it needs to be correlated with Paul's basic doctrine of union with Christ. The primitive teaching of the Church spoke of an objective transaction which critically altered the human situation and indeed the cosmos itself. It spoke of the decisive, irrevocable defeat of the principalities and powers of darkness. Yet we know that we ourselves are not whole, that there are areas of our life, and the life of the world, where the powers of darkness seem to be too much in the ascendant and we feel powerless to effect a change. If it was Christ's holiness, his complete unity with God, that really defeated the demons on Calvary, it could surely be that our chief problem is that we are only deficiently 'in Christ' and so incompletely in unity with God. All this makes it more difficult for us to join with Paul in his cry of faithful vulnerability, 'Wretched man that I am! Who will deliver me . . .', with sufficient emphasis upon the 'Thanks be to God through Jesus Christ our Lord!'[9]

When we lose our perception of the critical nature of the encounter between good and evil – an encounter that had its climax on the cross of Calvary – we lose not only the important element of struggle which is a natural part of every human life, but more seriously we lose our sense of the price paid for our salvation and the decisive nature of the encounter for ourselves and for the universe itself. From now on the powers of darkness are decisively defeated: 'He [God] disarmed the principalities and powers and made a public example of them, triumphing over them . . . in him [Christ]' (Colossians 2:15).

Now we know not only on which side we are entered but also what the ultimate outcome must be. There may be sporadic outbreaks of that demonic power but we know that the ultimate

power resides with God. As Jesus identified himself completely
with us in our human plight and predicament, so the Christian,
facing the principalities and powers, is now to identify with
Jesus in his sacrifice, his power and his victory. This is surely
what is meant by justification by faith. Not that we are justified
by our righteousness but by our response to the righteousness
of Christ – not by the position we have reached in our Christian
pilgrimage but by the 'set of the sails', the direction in which
we are travelling, by the fact that we have our faces towards
Christ and not our backs.

All this should assure us that the God with whom we have
to do in sickness and in health is the same God who was made
known to us in Jesus – in his incarnation, ministry, death and
glorious resurrection. That much sickness springs from sin is
not to be gainsaid. But it is not always possible to think of this
as a one-to-one consequence of personal sin, in the sense that
this particular action has led to this particular form of suffering.
He who died for us on the cross was without sin, and yet 'he
was wounded for our transgressions, he was bruised for our
iniquities . . . and with his stripes we are healed'.[10] In dealing
with sin on the cross, Christ has dealt with the root of sickness.
Suffering may still afflict us but it need not destroy us; for we
are to become 'more than conquerors through him who loved
us'.[11]

GOD AS RECONCILING LOVE

In Christ the divine promises are fulfilled and a new day has
dawned. Christ is the mediator of a new covenant in which the
world, formerly alienated from God, is now reconciled to God.
Christ is our health and salvation. In him alienation is changed
into at-one-ment. The prodigal is restored to the Father's house
with joy and celebration. From now on we know what it is to
be loved and to love in return; what it is to be human, for
Christ has taken our humanity and decked it out in glory.
Health, then, is that state of being in which we fully embody
the image of God, for God in Christ has shown us what we
were meant to be. Athanasius said: 'He became human that

we might become divine', or: he became what we are in order that we might become what he is.

This means that we must will what God has already willed, and indeed fulfilled, in Jesus Christ concerning sickness and all that is not good. We must work for the complete transformation of evil in whatever form it presents itself; but without demanding to know what the end will be. Sufficient for us to know that in various ways the serpent still makes his presence felt in the garden. The forbidden tree still bears fruit giving knowledge of good and evil. The road to infinite progress is also the road leading to great danger. The knowledge of nuclear power, for example, produces possibilities and dangers undreamed of by our forbears. It therefore requires of us greater and greater responsibility.

One of the first requirements of those involved in the healing ministry is an honest self-awareness and a readiness to acknowledge that we ourselves are not whole. The remedy is not just an earnest tidying up of ourselves or a periodic rush into 'spiritual discipline'. It is more a question of identifying ourselves with the younger brother in the story of the Prodigal, of recognising who, where and what we are. It is, in fact, an honest recognition of our own brokenness and alienation, and a determination to return to the Father's house in thankful recognition that healing grace is still available, 'grace to cover all my sin', as Charles Wesley put it. Paul describes this ongoing interaction of God with his world as reconciliation:

> Therefore, if any one is in Christ, he is a new creation; the old has passed away, behold, the new has come. All this is from God, who through Christ reconciled us to himself and gave us the ministry of reconciliation; that is, in Christ God was reconciling the world to himself, not counting their trespasses against them, and entrusting to us the message of reconciliation.[12]

When Leslie Tizard, one-time minister of Carrs Lane Church, Birmingham, lay dying of cancer, he said that at such a time there are not many things that seem to matter, but those few matter tremendously – far more than they ever did. What

seemed to him to be important at that time was contained in
St Paul's succinct summary of the gospel in those words: 'God
was in Christ reconciling the world to himself'. 'That *must* be
believed,' said Tizard, 'if I am to make any sense of the world
and of my own life in it.'[13]

Tizard was saying that in that situation above all others he
had to believe that there is a God who was revealed in Jesus
– in his life, his words, his works of healing, in his cross and
resurrection. For Christ is the one who has broken down the
dividing wall between ourselves and God and enabled us to
discover healing and renewal. In Christ God has crossed the
abyss to us in our sin, sickness, suffering and death, and taken
on our life in its disorder and disobedience and then given it
back to us in love. This same power to rescue and to heal,
located in Christ, is then entrusted to us. We are to 'heal the
sick, raise the dead, cleanse lepers, cast out demons'[14] within
the total context of going to make disciples of all nations.[15]

It is this reconciling character of God in Christ which under-
girds, authorises and energises the healing and caring mission
of the Church. One of the passages in the New Testament
which most clearly illustrates this for me comes in St John's
Gospel, where the writer describes the events of that first
Easter evening.[16] The disciples are meeting in the Upper Room,
we must suppose in Jerusalem. It is the promised day of the
Lord. But there is little sign of that for the moment. 'The
doors were shut', we are told, 'for fear of the Jews.' They are
overwhelmed with fear of what the authorities might do to
obliterate the memory of Jesus. So they crouch behind locked
doors.

Then, as he had promised to any two or three who gathered
in his name, Jesus was suddenly in their midst. The scars of
his passion are the signs by which they recognise him as their
Lord. He is the one from whom they had fled when the pressure
became too great; he whom one had betrayed and another
denied. But when he came among them there was no word of
reproach; just the gift of shalom, the gift which belonged to
the new age which he had promised. 'Peace be with you', he
said and then showed them his hands and his side, as if to
remind them of the tribulation which attends the work of the

Kingdom. So their fear was taken away and their sorrow was turned into joy. 'They were glad when they saw the Lord.'

Jesus said to them again: 'Peace be with you. As the Father has sent me, even so I send you.' When he had said this, he breathed on them and said: 'Receive the Holy Spirit', as though to give them the power and purpose for the mission. 'Ransomed, healed, restored, forgiven', they knew themselves called and equipped to be bearers of shalom to a stricken and suffering world. The process of redemption had begun. Like Schubert's Unfinished Symphony, or Barth's projected fifth volume of Dogmatics, it remains to others, and to us, to work towards its completion. The Kingdom of God has come. Praise the Lord! The best is yet to be, when the kingdom of this world has become the Kingdom of our Lord and of his Christ, and he shall reign for ever. Alleluia!

11

How Do We Care?

It was mainly for this purpose that Christ came, to wit, that
man might know how much God loves him; and that he
might learn this, to the intent that he might be enkindled to
the love of Him by whom he was first loved, and might also
love his neighbour.[1]

H. R. Mackintosh quotes these words of St Augustine in his
book, *The Christian Experience of Forgiveness*, a profound
attempt to interpret the atonement in terms of forgiveness.
After a careful study of forgiveness in terms of human life, in
terms of moral realities and in terms of divine forgiveness,
Mackintosh then looks at the implications of atonement in
terms of our own response to Christ through our relationship
with others. The crucifixion, he suggests, regarded purely as
an external historical event has no power to heal the human
heart. It must be manifested and reproduced in us. Its virtues
must mould our attitudes and actions, so that we become living
witnesses of the power of God's reconciling love in Christ. In
other words, the reality of the love of God in Jesus Christ can
best be seen in those who, having known the wonder of God's
grace, are themselves ready to forgive others; and the truth of
the atonement is most readily conveyed by those who have felt
the power of God's reconciling love in their own lives and are
concerned to express it in their relationship with others.

'Forgiveness,' he writes, 'is the experience by which we pass
from Christian truth to Christian duty.'[2] Though we may know
salvation in a personal and individual sense, we cannot enjoy
it fully except in a communal sense. Mackintosh continues:
'The content of the new morality inspired by forgiveness is

social in its constitutive essence. We cannot have God apart from our neighbour.'[3] So the pardoned have discovered that fellowship is the all-inclusive secret of human life and this means sharing our lives with all for whom God cares.

MEMBERS ONE OF ANOTHER

One of the working assumptions followed so far in this book is that we need to look more carefully at the corporate aspects of healing with its corollary that you cannot isolate the individual from the community and the sickness of that community. It is now more generally recognised that people are threatened by diseases of different origin:
(i) poverty-induced patterns of disease;
(ii) disease arising from disharmony within the natural environment;
(iii) disease arising from disharmony within the social environment.
In western society we are relatively free from poverty-induced forms of disease. We are now being warned about dangers of disharmony within the natural environment: the breaking-up of the ozone layer, pollution of the seas and rivers, and so on. For some years sociologists have advised of the dangers arising from disharmony within the social environment. An article in the *Guardian* newspaper some time ago came out with the banner headline 'Depression is a Social Disease'. There followed a report on the result of research which suggested that much depression amongst women springs from adverse life-events, lost or broken relationships.

The need for mutually supportive community groups where people can mix and meet and matter to one another is something that the churches have implicitly accepted for a long time. What we have not always done is to relate that to the best biblical, theological, medical and sociological thinking and ask *why* we are doing things in a certain way and whether, in the light of new understanding in these various disciplines, we might be doing them more effectively. So it is not only a question of *do* we care, but *how* do we care, and *why*? In what seems to be an increasingly depersonalised and depersonalising society the importance of that question cannot be overestimated.

I remember hearing Dr Murray Parkes tell of the occasion when his father was in hospital being prepared for a major operation. The senior consultant who was to perform the operation was one of the most skilled in that particular field in the whole country. But when he visited the old man, he treated him in rather a perfunctory manner, very much as an object rather than a person. When Murray Parkes visited later that day, the old man turned to his son in a rather distressed manner and said, 'He didn't seem as though he cared.' Murray Parkes suggested, 'Perhaps it is more important that he should know what he is doing.' As he looked, he saw tears come into the old man's eyes.

We begin with the belief that God is not only the Creator of life but also the determinant of all true values, the locus of community and that his essential nature is love. This means that human beings cannot be treated apart from a recognition of the society to which they belong, the moral and spiritual values of that society and the relationships within it. This has long been the basic assumption behind much of African society:

> To the African, a person is healthy if he is able to maintain moral uprightness, if he shows emotional maturity, and if he is able to maintain harmonious relationships within his family and with members of his community . . .
>
> Therefore, healing in the African concept involves physical, mental, social, emotional, moral and spiritual well-being. The social and emotional aspects of healing refer to good neighbourliness; while the spiritual aspect refers to harmonious relationships with one's ancestors, the local deities, and the Supreme Being. Consequently, to the African, healing is impossible in isolation: it is only possible in context; that is, within the sick person's community, which includes the living and the dead.[4]

Is it possible that we can learn from Africa and move towards a new moral and corporately-inspired underpinning for a spiritually enfeebled society? We certainly need to move away from that optical illusion of consciousness which enables us to see ourselves as distinct from others, and free to pursue our own course in separation and isolation from others. Every day we are being reminded that we can only live on this earth as members one of another, with a constant regard for what happens not only in our own family, community or nation, but what happens world-wide and within a total environment. This requires a complete transformation of spirituality which involves a widening of our circle of compassion to embrace all living creatures and the whole of nature in its beauty.

THE BASIC THEOLOGICAL CHALLENGE

The basic theological challenge is the challenge to love God and our neighbour as ourselves, and this is also the basis of the Church's diaconal, evangelical, missionary and medical tasks. It is a call and commission which cuts across all cultural and religious barriers, as we saw in Jesus' parable of the Good Samaritan. The Church's healing ministry must equally be directed not only to the whole person but to all people and the whole of creation. Modern theology based upon a corporate understanding of salvation points us to a kind of political holiness, to be realised by those who work to improve the quality of human life, to overcome racial and political injustice, for an end to the arms race and the arms trade, to care for the environment as part of God's creation. For this is God's world. In dealing with it we must start where Scripture begins, with creation. The ecologists and 'Greens' are already showing us the way. We must then move on to people – and to people we know and people who are round about us.

A particular example of this is the programme described as 'Community Care'. A Royal Commission in 1957 recommended that the mentally ill in Britain should be treated, as far as possible, on the same lines as those who are physically ill. This meant, in practical terms, that local authorities should be required to provide care outside hospital for the mentally impaired who did not need specialised treatment. Since 1981, the government has run down many of the old psychiatric hospitals and something like 70,000 former hospital patients have been discharged into the community. Some have settled satisfactorily into the community. Many will have found the loneliness and isolation more than they could bear. This has given rise to the slogan: 'Community care is fine so long as the community cares.' When it does not, then not only human happiness and well-being but also human lives are at risk.

So much depends upon the response that is made by individuals, by churches, by voluntary and statutory bodies. Is it surprising that in countries like Nigeria and Botswana, where the psychiatric service is not institutionally based but located in the community, community care works? This may be due in part to low population density, but also to the fact that there family and community relationships are given high priority and the community care programme is given higher financial priority by the government. Programmes like this emphasise the need for all of us, and not least those in the Christian churches, to give heed to the necessity consistently and with care 'to stand by' those who suffer, whether we can effect cure or not.

POLICIES AND PEOPLE

This might lead on to a consideration of the way in which our legislative structures, government policies and personal attitudes do in fact make people ill. It was no trendy left-wing parson but a theologian of world-wide repute, Karl Barth, who reminded us that the great questions about human health and well-being go far beyond the answers given by each of us individually. They are questions which require a corporate response. Barth writes:

They are social questions. Hygiene, sport and medicine arrive too late, and cannot be more than rather feeble palliatives, if such general conditions as wages, standards of living, working hours, necessary breaks, and above all housing are so ordered, or rather disordered, that instead of counteracting they promote and perhaps even cause illness, and therefore the external impairing of the will for life and health.[5]

Public health then is much too important a question to be left to the whim of the individual or the capricious wind of political change. In Britain we have recently celebrated the fortieth anniversary of the setting-up of the National Health Service. As with many human beings in their forties, the dear old NHS seems to be going through some kind of mid-life crisis. There are fewer and fewer of us about today who remember the old pre-1948 state of health care in this country. I cannot forget in my first days in the ministry visiting an old lady who was seriously ill with pneumonia. She lived on her own and was too afraid to send for the doctor in case she received a bill which she couldn't pay. I had to reassure her that now – this was in the latter part of 1950 – the attention she required would be provided under the NHS and would therefore be free of charge. Only then I was allowed to send for the doctor.

Prior to that we really did have a two-tier system of health care in which the poorest and the weakest were at a disadvantage. Many would agree with the eminent American who described the NHS as 'the finest bit of social legislation since the Magna Carta'. Many who initially opposed the setting-up of the Health Service in 1948, including most of the medical profession, have now come to see its value and are anxious that its essential structure should remain unchanged. This means that medical care should be available on the basis of need rather than the ability to pay.

Yet today, even though we pour into it something like ten per cent of our Gross National Product, the system seems to be breaking down. This is not because people do not care. There is perhaps no other sector of our society in which professionalism and the maintenance of high standards are so informed by compassion as our health-care system. Yet something has changed in society since 1948. For one thing, our values have changed. Our view of God has changed. Now, for the reconciling God of the Christian faith, we have substituted the God of success, growth and market forces. Our view of the person has changed, so that instead of thinking of individuals as unique, precious and mysterious beings made in the image and likeness of God, we think of them as body-machines, a curious combination of organs and tissues. I am reliably informed that medical students are given a good grounding in whole-person medicine during their first year of training but that in later years the excitement of high-technology medicine and the fascination of the analytical approach win the day. But perhaps the greatest factor is that the ability to supply a human need leads not to satiation but rather to increased expectation. This eventually leads to frustration in the never-ending battle for resources and then to weariness in well-doing in those called to supply that need. Little wonder then if the consumer is discomforted by what seem to be rushed, impersonal and uncaring attitudes in those called to care.

WEARINESS IN WELL-DOING

Anyone involved in the 'helping professions' or anyone who has been involved in bringing up a family is familiar with that feeling of complete exhaustion and inability to meet expectations. We know then that the essential question is not to know *when* to care and *how* to care, but how we as a family, as a health-care team, or as members of society, can *share* that burden of care more equally. The dangers of overactivity and anxiety are so great that some correctives have to be applied. One of these might be to remember that whilst, in measuring up to our own particular tasks, we have a responsibility *to* all, we cannot be expected to be responsible *for* all. We also need to remember that God always makes originals, not copies. What we have to offer is ourselves and we are unique. The effectiveness or otherwise of what we offer depends not so much upon the amount we achieve but the attitudes we reveal, the quality of the decisions we make and the way in which in all this we reflect Christ's presence: in other words, by what we *are* rather than what we *do*. Most of us are painfully aware that in the doing we can become so exhausted that we deny the truth of what we *are*. Then we just have to slow down so that we may more faithfully make known Christ's presence and thus his care and compassion.

Bob Lambourne confessed how, as a GP in Birmingham, in sheer fatigue, he sometimes found himself just going through the motions. He wrote:

> Dragged out of bed in the middle of the night with nothing but resentment in my heart, it happened on several occasions, I rebuked my disinclination to give proper attention to some unattractive person and to make a thorough examination. I rebuked myself with the remembrance of Christ's word, 'Ye did it unto me', and then it suddenly seemed that Christ was really and literally present under my hands in the form of the sick person. I saw him and I touched him.[6]

We should never underestimate the healing power of listening or of the quiet foot-washing exercise. As Jesus taught so plainly in the Gospel story of Martha and Mary, the charge to love need not always project us into a maelstrom of feverish activity in which the central principle of love may become dangerously diminished. More important is the quality of our giving and the depth and character of our love.

THE 'ALREADY' AND THE 'NOT YET'

We do need the great prophetic figures like Martin Luther King, Archbishop Romero, Archbishop Tutu and others who will defy those who try to domesticate Christianity and deny its prophetic role. They stand as powerful examples to us all, as shining lights in a darkling world. In their own critical and courageous way they reflect Christ's presence in the world. We may not all be able to follow them in the costly way they have chosen, but we can learn from them just what it means to live in that creative tension between the 'already' and the 'not yet' of Christian faith. Already Christ has come, the Holy Spirit has been given, but we do not yet see all things brought to perfection. So we are called to live in hope. Christian hope, which like 'love' is a strong word, is not based upon any optimism about human nature but about what God has done, is capable of doing and will do with our less-than-perfect selves. In the meantime, as Paul reminded us, we are to be 'imitators of God . . . and walk in love, as Christ loved us and gave himself up for us, a fragrant offering and sacrifice to God'.[7] The kind of love that Paul was here describing involves recognition of the needs and rights of others, consideration, trust, deep sympathy, fidelity through success and failure, through grief and sorrow, and the readiness, if need be, to sacrifice for others.

'Who is man?' asked a Jewish writer. 'A being in travail with God's dreams and designs.' And he went on to say, 'How embarrassing to be a messenger who forgot the message.' We may not have a ready solution to all the problems that face us, we may sometimes be so overwhelmed by the travail that we cannot always deliver the message clearly or embody it completely. We should understand that this is a normal situation in any biblical understanding of the people of God. But we must not forget the message: 'God so loved the world that he gave his only Son.' His purpose was 'through him to reconcile to himself all things, whether on earth or in heaven, making peace through the blood of his cross'. The only way in which this total and unlimited responsibility is to be accepted, or can be accepted, is in and through the grace of God. We are not sufficient for these things, but he is sufficient. If we are not to give way to dangerous fantasies of omnipotence, or alternatively to destructive feelings of despair, we must clearly understand that our sufficiency must be in him.

It was a black American churchman, from the same mould as Martin Luther King, Dr Benjamin Mays, who said:

The tragedy of life does not lie in not reaching your goal. The tragedy lies in having no goal to reach. It isn't a calamity to die with dreams unfulfilled, but it is a calamity not to dream. It is not a disaster to be unable to capture your ideal, but it is a disaster to have no ideal to capture. It is not a disgrace not to reach the stars, but it is a disgrace to have no stars to reach for. Not failure but low aim is sin.

We Christians are a wayfaring people and we have to learn with Calvin that 'it is better to limp along the path of God's way than to dash with all speed outside it'. We are on a difficult and hazardous journey, an exploration into wholeness, an exploration into God. Our ultimate care and concern then is with

> What no eye has seen, nor ear heard,
> nor the heart of man conceived,
> what God has prepared for those who love him.[8]

Robbed of this wisdom, the wisdom of love, the wisdom of God, then we are in danger of missing the point, following false gods and wandering in a wilderness which provides no entrance to the promised land.

Notes

CHAPTER 1: HEALING MINISTRY IN THE CHURCH TODAY

1. Howard T. Somervell, *After Everest*. Hodder and Stoughton 1936, pp. 259–60.
2. Ministry of Healing: Report of Committee appointed according to Resolution 63 of Lambeth Conference, 1930, pp. 61ff.
3. Anthony Bird, *The Search for Health, A Response from the Inner City*. Department of Theology, Birmingham.
   Michael Wilson, *A Coat of Many Colours – Pastoral Studies of the Christian Way of Life*. Epworth 1988.
4. A. Graham Ikin, *New Concepts of Healing*. Hodder and Stoughton 1955.
5. Luke 23:46.

CHAPTER 2: HEALING IN THE BIBLICAL TRADITION

1. William Watty, *Man and Healing*. Caribbean Regional Conference on the Churches' Role in Health and Wholeness, Port of Spain, 1979, p. 7. Published by Christian Medical Commission, W.C.C., Geneva.
2. Genesis 1:31.
3. Deuteronomy 32:39, Jerusalem Bible, Darton, Longman and Todd.
4. Exodus 15:26.
5. Genesis 17:17–21.
6. 1 Kings 17:17–23; 2 Kings 4:18–37.
7. 2 Kings 5:1–14.
8. Job 2:3.
9. Hans Küng, *On Being a Christian*. Collins 1976, p. 231.
10. Matthew 10:7–8.
11. Matthew 12:27–8.

12. Matthew 11:4–5.
13. Luke 4:18–21.
14. Mark 10:52; Mark 5:34; Matthew 9:29.
15. Mark 2:5.
16. Mark 6:5.
17. Mark 7:33–4; 8:23.
18. John 11:43; Luke 17:14; Mark 5:8; John 4:50.
19. Lesslie Newbigin, *The Light Has Come*. Wm. B. Eerdmans 1982, p. 119.
20. John Marsh, *St John*. Pelican New Testament Commentaries. Penguin Books 1968, 1971 and 2, p. 378.
21. Luke 13:2–5.
22. Matthew 12:44–5.
23. James 5:13–15.
24. Arnold Bittlinger, *Spiritual Healing in the Bible Today*, Report on Seminar on The Healing Ministry of the Church, Ecumenical Institute, Bossey, 1979, p. 1.
25. 2 Corinthians 12:8–9.
26. John 14:12.
27. Revelation 22:2.

CHAPTER 3: HEALING AS INTEGRATION

1. Helen Chappell, 'Third Person', *The Guardian*, 15 February 1989.
2. Juvenal, *Satyre X*, 1.356.
3. Margaret Whitehead, *The Health Divide – Inequalities in Health in the 1980's*. Health Education Council 1987.
4. F. W. Dillistone, *The Christian Understanding of Atonement*. Nisbet 1968, p. 2.
5. Morton T. Kelsey, *Healing and Christianity*. SCM Press Ltd 1973, p. 248.
6. 1 Corinthians 15:22.
7. Bob Lambourne, *Explorations in Health and Salvation*, ed. M. Wilson. University of Birmingham 1983, pp. 19–20.
8. William Watty, *Man and Healing – A Biblical and Theological View*, Christian Medical Commission, W.C.C., Caribbean Regional Conference, Trinidad 1979, p. 12.
9. Philippians 4:4ff.
10. Wm. A. R. Thompson, *Faiths That Heal*. A. and C. Black Ltd 1980, p. 198.

11. Morton T. Kelsey, *Healing and Christianity*. SCM Press Ltd 1973, p. 247.
12. Wm. A. R. Thompson, *Faiths That Heal*. A. and C. Black Ltd 1980, p. 201.
13. Matthew 12:25.
14. Mark 2:1–12.
15. Grace Jantzen, *Julian of Norwich*. SPCK 1987, p. 206.

CHAPTER 4: HEALING MIRACLES

1. Matthew 17:24–7.
2. Ibid 4:3ff.
3. Augustine, *The City of God*, tr. John Healey. Everyman's Library 1950, vol. ii, p. 329.
4. D. C. Westerman, *Salvation and Healing in the Community, The Old Testament Understanding*. International Review of Missions, 1971.
5. 2 Kings 5.
6. Peter Ackroyd, *The Times*, Review, 24 December 1988.

CHAPTER 5: MANY FACES, MANY FORMS

1. Philippians 2:12–13.
2. William Robinson, *The Shattered Cross*. Berean Press 1953, p. 73.
3. Janet Marshall, *Good Housekeeping*, March 1988.
4. 2 Corinthians 12:7–10.
5. Paul Tillich, *Systematic Theology*, vol. iii, pp. 278–9.
6. M. A. H. Melinsky, *Healing Miracles*. A. R. Mowbray 1968, pp. 166–7.
7. Evelyn Frost, *Christian Healing*. A. R. Mowbray 1949, p. 159.
8. 2 Corinthians 4:6.
9. Quoted by Charlotte Saikovski in article 'Christian Healing Today' in *Christian Science Monitor Special Report* 1988.
10. Isaiah 53:4.
11. Romans 8:32.
12. Bob Lambourne, *Explorations in Health and Healing*. University of Birmingham 1983, p. 83.
13. 1 Corinthians 12–14.

CHAPTER 6: SUFFERING AND A GOD OF LOVE

1. Luke 13:1–5.
2. Matthew 10:29.
3. Isaiah 63:9 and 53:4.
4. Psalm 27:13.
5. Job 42:5.
6. Genesis 19:30–8.
7. Isaiah 53:5ff.
8. Martin Camroux, *Reform*, April 1988.
9. Dietrich Bonhoeffer, *The Way to Freedom*. Collins, third impression 1982, p. 251.
10. Romans 8:35ff.
11 For further discussion of this see Grace Jantzen, *Julian of Norwich*. SPCK 1987. Chapter 10, Spiritual Growth and Healing.
12. *Julian of Norwich: Showings*, Classics of Western Spirituality. London SPCK and Paulist Press, New York 1978. The long text.
13. Bob Lambourne, *Explorations in Health and Salvation*, ed. Michael Wilson. University of Birmingham 1983, p. 28.
14. Galatians 4:13–14.
15. 2 Corinthians 12:9.

CHAPTER 7: HEALING AND THE LOCAL CHURCH

1. *The Healing Church*, World Council of Churches Report. Geneva 1965.
2. Malcolm Muggeridge, *Something Beautiful for God*. Collins 1971, p. 119.
3. Mark 16:20.
4. Acts 3:16.
5. Acts 5:12.
6. Acts 5:15.
7. Luke 7:16.
8. Gerald Caplan, *An Approach to Community Health*. Tavistock Publications 1961, p. 138.
9. 1 Corinthians 12:21.
10. Lesslie Newbigin, 'The Pastor's Opportunities, Evangelism in the City', *The Expository Times*, September 1987, T. and T. Clark, Edinburgh.
11. Matthew 22:37–9.
12. 1 John 4:10.

CHAPTER 8: HEALING PRAYER

1. Acts 2:42–3 (New English Bible).
2. *Health and Healing – A Study Kit*, United Reformed Church, 1982, edited by the author and for which he wrote. (He is grateful for the opportunity to be able to reproduce briefly some of the material he wrote then.)
3. Leslie D. Weatherhead, *Psychology, Religion and Healing*. Hodder and Stoughton, 1951, p. 376.
4. 1 Corinthians 15:22.
5. John Richards, *The Question of Healing Services*. Daybreak, Darton, Longman and Todd 1989, p. 102.
6. Mark 6:12–13.
7. Raphael Frost osb, *Christ and Wholeness*. James Clarke and Co. 1985, p. 61.
8. John Calvin, *Institutes of the Christian Religion*, IV, 19–20.
9. 2 Corinthians 1:3–4.

CHAPTER 9: TOWARDS A WORKING THEOLOGY

1. Isaiah 61:1–2; Luke 4:18–19.
2. P. T. Forsyth, *The Cruciality of the Cross*. Independent Press 1948, pp. 81–2.
3. Findings of the Tübingen Consultation 1964, *The Healing Church*, p. 35.
4. Ibid.
5. John 9:17.
6. John 14:10.
7. Donald Baillie, *God was in Christ*. Faber 1956, p. 205.
8. The New Testament in English, John Wycliffe (AD 1380, revised by John Purvey, c. 1388, reprinted Oxford, Clarendon Press 1879. The writer is grateful to the Rev. Dr J. Walter Houston of Westminster College, Cambridge, for examining the original documents.)
9. Romans 8:22–4.
10. Romans 8:38–9.
11. Colossians 1:19–20.
12. Luke 19:1–10.
13. 2 Corinthians 4:8ff, The Jerusalem Bible.
14. 1 Thessalonians 5:23.
15. Miles Parkinson, *In Gear*, September 1988.
16. Matthew 10:8.

17. *Whole Person Medicine*, Report to R.C.G.P. and C.C.H.H., 1988, in the writing of which the present author was considerably involved, pp. 20–1.
18. Luke 17:11–19.
19. Eustus Evans, *Pastoral Care in a Changing World*. Epworth 1961, p. 98.
20. Morton T. Kelsey, *Healing and Christianity*. SCM Press Ltd 1973, p. 224.
21. Matthew 7:7.
22. Matthew 7:11.

CHAPTER 10: THE GOD WHO HEALS

1. Genesis 3:8.
2. Genesis 3:19.
3. Hosea 11:1–9.
4. Hebrews 1:1–3a.
5. Romans 7:19–20.
6. James Denney, *Romans*, E.G.T., pp. 641–2. Quoted by Professor James Stewart in his paper 'On a Neglected Emphasis in New Testament Theology', *Scottish Journal of Theology*, vol. 4, September 1951, p. 292.
7. Karl Barth, *Church Dogmatics*, vol. III, part 4, p. 368.
8. James Stewart, op. cit., 'On a Neglected Emphasis in New Testament Theology'.
9. Romans 7:24–5.
10. Isaiah 53:5.
11. Romans 8:37.
12. 2 Corinthians 5:17–19.
13. Leslie J. Tizard, *Facing Life and Death*. George Allen and Unwin, 1959, p. 150.
14. Matthew 10:8.
15. Matthew 28:19.
16. John 20:19–22.

CHAPTER 11: HOW DO WE CARE?

1. H. R. Mackintosh, *The Christian Experience of Forgiveness*. Collins, Fontana 1961, p. 180.
2. Ibid. p. 217.

3. Ibid. p. 230.
4. Christian Medical Commission, World Council of Churches. African Regional Conference on the Churches' Role in Health and Wholeness. Gabarone, Botswana, 1979, p. 37.
5. Karl Barth, *Church Dogmatics*, vol. III, part 4, p. 363.
6. A. van Soest, *Bob Lambourne*. Sermon at Bob Lambourne's Memorial Service. D.P.S. Spring School Papers, Theology Department, University of Birmingham, 1972.
7. Ephesians 5:1–2.
8. 1 Corinthians 2:9.

Index